INTO FEZ

Tourism, Tourists and Tour Guides in an Urban Moroccan Demimonde

Jesse A. Dizard

KENDALL/HUNT PUBLISHING COMPANY
4050 Westmark Drive   Dubuque, Iowa 52002

Cover image © Shutterstock

Copyright © 2008 by Kendall/Hunt Publishing Company

ISBN 978-0-7575-5504-6

All rights reserved. No part of this publication may be reproduced, stored in a retrieval system, or transmitted, in any form or by any means, electronic, mechanical, photocopying, recording, or otherwise, without the prior written permission of the copyright owner.

Printed in the United States of America
10 9 8 7 6 5 4 3 2 1

*To my mother, father, wife and daughters;
thank you for everything, without your love
I could never have survived.*

CONTENTS

A Note on Dialogue vii

Acknowledgements ix

Introduction xi

Chapter 1   Tradition and Modernity in Fez, Morocco 1

Chapter 2   Inarticulate Resentment 7

Chapter 3   Tour Guides 13

Chapter 4   Finding Fez 29

Chapter 5   Failure Considered and Reconsidered 35

Chapter 6   Meeting My Baker 41

Chapter 7   Driss, the Weaver 47

Chapter 8   Righteous Men of God Defying the Power of
             an Unjust Ruler 49

Chapter 9   Unmet Expectations 55

Chapter 10   The Nature of Authenticity 67

Chapter 11   Seeking Authenticity 73

Chapter 12   Open Sesame 79

Chapter 13   The Animal and the Scorpion 83

Chapter 14   The Lynx 89

Chapter 15   Al Malik 95

Chapter 16   The Context of Suspicion 99

Chapter 17   Learning to be Useful 103

Chapter 18   Working for the Lynx 105

Chapter 19	Entranced	119
Chapter 20	Unraveling	123
Chapter 21	Refractions of Reflections on Fieldwork in Morocco: Postmodernity, or the Sibylline	127
Chapter 22	So What?	131
	Study Questions	135
	Bibliography	143

A NOTE ON DIALOGUE

> *As a way to arrive at the truth, exactitude and methodology are, in the end, far inferior to vision and apotheosis*
>
> —Mark Helprin (1992:30)

All my original fieldnotes were lost when my computer, into which I had recorded detailed descriptions of my days in Fez, was stolen from my car in Milwaukee, Wisconsin in July of 1995. Some secondary notebooks were not stolen, nor were my memories— though many I have tried diligently to forget. Therefore, the conversations to which I have occasion to refer, as well as the sustained commentaries from various informants, are not all verbatim. Some are approximations, some "individuals" are composites drawn from several of the people I came to know, and some descriptions are reconstructed from a variety of the events I experienced. I do not think this poses much of a problem, for even had my original descriptions not been lost, I would have been unwilling to use the exact words of my informants for fear of compromising their personal safety. Though the conurbation that is modern Fez is a relatively large city (roughly one million inhabitants), it is still a small town when it comes to the seemingly boundless paranoia of the Alaouite monarchy. Though I was devastated by the loss of my notes at the time, in retrospect I find that it was all for the best. I do wonder, however, just who wound up with that computer, and what if anything they thought of its contents, or if they even bothered to read them at all…

ACKNOWLEDGEMENTS

This work would not have been possible without the generous help of many, many people, especially the Moroccans who took time to explain their lives to me. I cannot name them individually, but they know who they are. I would also like to thank the Fulbright Commission for their generous support. Mary Pete made a place for me where others would not; 'Quyana.' My profound gratitude and respect are also due to Gerald Berreman, Laura Nader, and Richard Ofshe, three paragons of intellection, compassion and virtue in a harsh and unforgiving landscape. Finally, I would like to acknowledge the contributions of my students and colleagues in Oregon, Alaska, and California; they asked me many questions and forced me to think more carefully in order to answer them.

All errors of omission and commission are mine alone.

INTRODUCTION

> *"Indeed, God does not guide the wicked people."*
>
> —AL QUR'AN

I spent a total of 13 months in Fez, Morocco learning the ways of Fez's unofficial tour guides. It is a dangerous job. The guides face jail, extortion, or worse, in addition to the demands of honor and identity that all young Moroccan men and women face. The guides I met survive by forming syndicates which afford some protection, but also create new demands. The group I came to know is essentially a mutual assistance association drawn from neighborhoods and families in which informal control mechanisms have deteriorated or disappeared altogether. The guide is awash in an ocean of relatively wealthy foreigners who are able to sample the planet's cultures as from a box of chocolates. Tourists consume what they take to be the finest the guides' own society affords, paying often exorbitant sums (in relative terms) for so-called peak experiences which none of my informants could ever have afforded, were they not someone's guide.

What is it like to guide, translating bits and pieces of one's own social and material culture to foreigners? How much, and how accurately does one translate or explain matters of interest or mere curiosity to one's client? I never heard a guide say, "I don't know." In a society of long-standing antipathy towards outsiders, how well or badly do the guides maintain their status as outsider's insiders? Is reality really bargained for? What is hidden from outsiders and why? What risks do guides actually run?

The deviant behavior the guides display is contributing to an on-going struggle over the definition of contemporary Islam in Morocco. There is great anxiety and controversy over which direction Moroccan society will go. One option is that it will accommodate modernity, in spite of its *jahilyya* and what Ritzer (2000) has called the McDonaldization of society. Or, the fear is that Morocco will fall prey to what Kepel (1994) has called an evangelical form of Islam. By dubious virtue of their liminal position within the demimonde of Fez, the guides are at the sharp end of a wedge driving into the heart of Moroccan society.

Paul Bowles (1991) has described Fez as a singularly unhealthful place. I would be hard-pressed to disagree. And yet despite the noisome smells, the pallid complexions, the poverty and overcrowding, I found a vigorous and robust quality to the people who guided me through their world. Because of the dislocation their families have experienced, and the often grinding poverty in which they were raised, and in which many continue to live, the guides I knew were sensitive, thoughtful, and tough. Yet they were also fatalistic, mournful, and tragic souls.

Despite my accented Arabic, my status as an outsider, and my ambiguous reasons for being there, a notorious group of guides accepted me as one of their own, showed me their world, introduced me to allies, alerted me to enemies, and patiently explained the convoluted network of relationships necessary for survival in Fez's narrow alleys. Ultimately, I "passed": I became a member of their *confrèrie* and spent many hours sharing stories and other pleasures with them. I guided foreign tourists. I "earned" commissions. I was nearly arrested.

Acceptance was perhaps never more than partial however. I was useful; therefore, I was tolerated and, on occasion, confided in. A *quid pro quo* was always either explicit or implicit in all our interactions.

To guide successfully is—among many things—a matter of controlling one's clients' means of maintaining an adequate definition of reality. According to the Oxford English Dictionary, one of the earliest contextual definitions (ca. 1585) of the English verb "to guide" suggests origins in the Arabic *qada'u*: "He which is the guide goeth before mounted on a camel." Hans Wehr (1980) offers the following translation of the Arabic: "To lead, lead by a halter; conduct, engineer, steer; to drive (a car), pilot (an airplane); to pander, pimp; to be led, to follow, obey, yield, submit, retaliate." Explicit in the Arabic are the binary oppositions of control and submission, delinquency and conformity, resistance and placidity. "I know," one guide told me. "We kill ourselves with our own hands."

CHAPTER 1

Tradition and Modernity in Fez, Morocco

> *By Tradition I do not mean the docile transmission of some dead deposit, but rather the living repetition that manages to suggest a fresh truth. There is no such thing as a tradition that exists of its own accord. Instead, and always, tradition has to be embraced and cultivated.*
>
> —DEMETRI PORPHYRIOS (2002)

> *Tradition by definition, is the inherited and complex evolution of things cultural, social, conventional, and institutional. The question regarding it is: which traditions live and change, and which do not.*
>
> —DUNCAN MCCALLUM MCROBERTS (2002)

> *In an opening address {for a} colloquium on "the Kingdom of Morocco between tradition and modernity," Moroccan Prime Minister, Abderrahmane Youssoufi, surveyed the changes underway in the kingdom that are geared towards the establishment of "political, economic and social modernity," saying Morocco is operating these changes "in its own way, at its own pace," and that while doing so it sticks to its identity and peculiarities.*
>
> —WWW.ARABICNEWS.COM (19 JUNE 2000)

I had never thought much about the people of North Africa, let alone Morocco, until I read *Les Boucs*[1] (1955) by Driss Chraïbi for

---

[1] The English translation is *The Butts: A Novel*.

an undergraduate seminar on post-colonial francophone literature. The novel is a searing examination of racism towards North African immigrants in France. It made an impression on me because, as a student of French literature, I had only read the classics: Racine, Molière, de Maupassant, Hugo, Balzac, et cetera. Even Zola's novels of 19th century misery were not so harsh, so bitter. What had France done to deserve such vituperation, I wondered? A history professor handed me a copy of Horne's *A Savage War of Peace: Algeria 1954–1962* (1977). This was followed by Céline's *Voyage au bout de la nuit*[2] (1932), a section of which describes conditions in a French West African colony similar to those found in Conrad's *Heart of Darkness*. It was *schadenfreude* perhaps, but I proceeded to read every piece of contemporary fiction from North Africa, especially Morocco, that I could find. A year later I went to the *Université de la Sorbonne* in Paris to study literature and philosophy. While there I met many people from former French colonies in Africa. I especially enjoyed the Moroccans because they were particularly irreverent and acerbic.[3]

I had enrolled in a seminar on philosophy taught by a man in whose work I had become interested before leaving for Paris. Jacques Derrida, a North African of *pied noir* origins,[4] was an eloquent lecturer, if abstract. After several hours each week spent bemused and confused, I would seek the company of my Moroccan friends whose pragmatism was a relief from the philosopher's peculiar questions such as, "What is the structure of the area of this poem by Paul Célan?" And when it came to language,

---

[2]The English translation is *Journey to the End of the Night*.

[3]One day, I was talking with a Moroccan man lounging near Daviod's Fountain of Saint Michael at the Place St. Michel. I'll call him Ahmed. He asked if I wanted to smoke hashish with him, producing a small lump of it that had been tucked inside his mouth. "Right here on the plaza?" I asked, incredulous. "Sure," replied Ahmed. I expressed reservations, after all there are gendarmes who might frown on such behavior in public; just then one was walking towards us. "Gendarmes!" He contemptuously spat out the word. "They are stupid. Watch." As the officer approached, Ahmed tossed the hashish onto the sidewalk, directly in the path of the oncoming gendarme. He walked right past us, even looking me in the eyes. A moment later, Ahmed casually bent down, regained control of his substance, and proceeded to fashion the most extraordinary cigarette fraught with impurities.

[4]*Pied noir* is the term for French colonists in Algeria.

the same practical attitude made for some hilarious fun at the expense of the notorious ambiguity of French. For example, the word *vraiment*, which means "truly," "really," or "verily" can be disarticulated into two parts, *vrai*, "true" and *ment*, the adverbial suffix. But *ment* also sounds exactly like the verb "to lie" conjugated in the second person singular. So, my Moroccan friend posed the following question: *"Vraiment? Comment peut le vrai mentir?"* (Verily? How can the truth lie?). This struck me as a suitable reply to Professor Derrida's exceedingly abstract query.

Several years later, in 1987, I went to North Africa on something of a quest. I had received a Watson Fellowship to investigate the relationships between language and political independence, culture and colonialism, in the former French colonies of North and West Africa. In short, I wondered why do African novelists continue to compose in French? That undergraduate seminar on post-colonial French literature had succeeded in planting questions more enduring, in my view, than those of the famous philosopher. Before visiting Fez, I spent some time in Casablanca, Marrakesh, and Rabat listening to novelists and poets share with me their metaphors. Each in their own way, they taught me that the traditional world, the way of life that colonialism sought to modernize, had not disappeared. Rather modernity was like a layer of something under which remains the substrate of tradition, and occasionally tradition is visible beneath the folds of the modern world.

But, I wondered, what exactly is "tradition"? According to *Black's Law Dictionary* (Garner 1999:1495), Tradition is defined as "Past customs and usages which influence or govern present acts or practices." However, there is also reference to the Latin "traditio," which, in civil law means delivery, or transfer of possession; "a derivative mode of acquiring, by which the owner of a corporeal thing, having the right and the will of aliening it, transfers it for a lawful consideration to the receiver." Another source, *Bouvier's Legal Dictionary* (www.lectlaw.com, 2002), defines tradition as "The act by which a thing is delivered by one or more persons to one or more others." In addition,

> *Tradition is either real or symbolical. The first is where the* ipsa corpora *of movables are put into the hands of the receiver. Symbolical tradition is used where the thing is incapable of real delivery, as in immovable subjects such as*

> *lands and houses; or such as consist* in jure *(things incorporeal) as things of fishing and the like. The property of certain movables, though they are capable of real delivery, may be transferred by symbol. Thus, if the subject be under lock and key, the delivery of the key is considered as a legal tradition of all that is contained in the repository.*

Not only is tradition a matter of transferring something from one to another individual or group, the thing itself may be symbolic of both the transfer and of the tradition. The traditional (act, object, ritual, utterance, etc) can be symbolic and it can be symbolized by something else.

Edward Shils defines tradition more broadly as essentially "a traditium; it is anything which is transmitted or handed down from the past to the present" (1981:12). Further, Shils maintains that while tradition can and does change, the central features or core basis for the traditions' existence remains with the context intact (1981:13, 19). Taking issue with this, Handler and Lennekin (1989) argue that "tradition is a model of the past and is inseparable from the interpretation of tradition in the present" (1989:41). This definition insists that tradition can be modified by those who perpetuate it. Because of such alterations, even the core basis of the tradition can become "corrupted" with new material. Therefore, tradition is fundamentally of symbolic rather than natural constitution (1989: 41), bringing us closer to the legal definition. It is what Professor Derrida might call "a shibboleth," the password of belonging and cultural identity.

"Modern" then is the contemporary iteration of "tradition" in whatever form local particularism prefers. "Modernity" therefore is not really a period of time at all. Rather, it describes the constellation of processes and conditions associated with bureaucracies, capitalism, industrial technology, and Weberian rationality. "Postmodern" would, by further extension, imply whatever comes after that which is "modern"—or rather, that which is the contemporary version of "tradition." Somewhat confused, I went to Fez for the first time.

In Fez the full force of the maelstrom was apparent: behavior resisted neat categorization as "modern" or "traditional" or "postmodern." Here tradition and modernity interpenetrated, here postmodernity seemed to be a tangible, palpable reality. The stark juxtaposition of the walled city, *Fès al-bali*, with the *Ville Nouvelle*, made the distinction between modern and traditional seem obvious.[5] The *Ville Nouvelle* boasts billboards, broad boulevards, boutiques, apartment buildings, and wide sidewalks. *Fès al-bali* within its crenellated walls feels medieval—there are no roads, only narrow alleyways; donkeys carry all goods and supplies in and out of the old city, and one must watch one's step to avoid the slippery evidence of a mule-train's passage. To see a man dressed in a suit and tie was quite normal in the *Ville Nouvelle*, but the same man dressed that way in *Fès al-bali* seemed out of place, even alien, given his surroundings. Veiled women looked equally odd in the *Ville Nouvelle*, whereas in *Fès al-bali*, they seemed more appropriate to the context: a traditional costume in its traditional milieu.

My confusion about what was modern, and what was traditional, grew greater the longer I lingered in Fez. The view from a rooftop in *Fès al-bali* proved disorienting, further upsetting the apple-cart of categories: I saw many satellite dishes, electrical wires strung from odd angles, as well as the occasional ram hobbled on a roof, being fattened for the *eid al-kebir* celebrating the end of *Ramadan*. In 1987 the coexistence of satellite television and veiled women seemed as profoundly contradictory as Palestinian teens hurling paving stones at the Israeli Defense Forces soldiers during the first *Intifada*.

One day while wandering through *Fès al-bali* I watched a wedding procession pass. The bride was borne upon a beautiful palanquin, dressed in rich brocades, her hands stained with a filigree pattern of henna. She was surrounded by crowds of ululating women, each of whom had henna-stained hands as well—though none as elaborately done as those of the bride. "How authentic, how very traditional," I thought to myself as the procession approached. But as the crowd drew near I noticed that the bride was not Moroccan. She was Japanese, and so was her groom. The musicians and

---

[5]The conurbation that is modern Fez (or *Fès* in French orthography) can be divided into five sections: *Fès al-bali*, the old city—also known colloquially as *al medina*; *Fès J'did*, the new city—dating from the 13th century Merinide Dynasty; the Jewish quarter, *al mellah*; the French colonial *Ville Nouvelle*, built outside the ancient walls; and the recently erected *bidonvilles* and temporary shelters of the poor.

well-wishers had been hired by the couple to provide them with a real Moroccan wedding experience! Clearly, under specific circumstances and within particular contexts ceremony, clothing, and comestibles are only superficial indicators of cultural complexity.

To further complicate matters, a small army of young men besieged the Euro-American visitor offering their services as guides to *Fès al-bali* and its sights, hidden within the labyrinthine network of alleyways. Inevitably, after a short tour of the most famous and picturesque aspects of *Fès al-bali,* the visitor is led to a carpet shop and offered the opportunity to purchase an authentic, hand-made rug or Berber blanket. The modern guides sell tradition to postmodern tourists.

Is this behavior modern? Postmodern? Or is it traditional? I went back to Fez in 1993 to try to find out more about the interpenetration of tradition, modernity, and postmodernity.

CHAPTER 2

Inarticulate Resentment

"Hey they don't like our jokes? Well, if they don't like our jokes, what are they going to do when we are serious?" [6]

New crusades are taking shape. Yet oddly, as American Evangelicals denounce Islam as "evil,"[7] and calls for holy war in defense of Islam ring out from *mihrab* (the niche in a mosque's wall indicating the direction of Mecca) after *mihrab*, these new crusades are a conflict within Islam itself. The contest is for neither land nor faith, but rather for the definition of modern Islam. In the midst of strident calls for jihad,[8] ethnic cleansing, and the rapture of end times, trade continues, even flourishes. As "McWorld" jousts with "Tribalism" (Barber 1996), tickets to the contest are being sold.

Every Muslim country, in a great arc from Senegal in the West to Egypt and across Asia to the Indonesian archipelago, seems to claim a "holy city of Islam." Unlike the others, however (except

---

[6] New York Times, 21, February 1995, "Casablanca Journal; Jokes From Underground Keep Morocco Laughing" by Chris Hedges.
[7] *New York Times*, 27 May 2003, "Seeing Islam as 'Evil' Faith, Evangelicals Seek Converts."
[8] Strictly defined, *jihad* is a holy war or spiritual struggle against infidels. See *Al-Qur'an*, Surah 9, subsection 41: "O believers, go out in the cause of God (*jahidu*), whether light or heavy, and strive in the service of God, wealth and soul. This is better for you if you understand." Additionally, *jihad* has been interpreted to mean an individual's internal spiritual struggle against vice, passion, and ignorance.

perhaps Cairo with its *Al Azhar* university), the ramparts surrounding the labyrinth that is Fez guard—among other things—the oldest Islamic university in the world at the *Al Quarawiyyine* mosque. It was founded with the city itself roughly 200 years after the Prophet Mohammed's death.

Not only does Fez attract serious pious men to study at the feet of orthodox *fquih* (Muslim theologians) at *Al Quarawiyyine*, but also, like every other major urban area in the world, it has a large number of impoverished people eking out an existence on the margins of modernity's cornucopia. I assumed that, having grown up without running water or electricity, nor hope for an education, from among these people are recruited the soldiers of terrorist armies like *Al Qaida* or Morocco's *al-Assirat el Moustaqim*[9], *al- 'Adl w-al-Ihsan* (Justice and Charity) et cetera.[10] Indeed, from among Fez's poor also come the hustlers I got to know so well. Curiously, however, I discovered quite the contrary: while I encountered widespread resentment, cynicism, and resignation, I found little evidence for a will-to-violence directed at foreign tourists generally, or even Americans in particular.

The twentieth century has been the Age of Hatred, an amplification of ancient enmities. More specifically, while secularism has clearly been a dominant force and has, along with globalizing economic pressures, reshaped national cultures, it is nevertheless also the case that local affections and ethnic and religious identities have been remarkably durable. But while some Muslim states (Iran, Sudan, and Syria for example) are being defined as enemies of democracy for jingoistic nationalist ends, even as capital becomes increasingly interdependent, demonstrating little use for nationalism, it must be understood that for the vast majority of Muslims this anger is not directed at a culture—Euro-American or

---

[9]*Assirat el Moustaqim*, literally "The Straight Path," has been named by Morocco's State Prosecutor as the primary organization responsible for the May 16, 2003 bombings in Casablanca which killed 45 people.

[10]One year after the September 11th attacks, a State Department report argued that development aid should be based "on the belief that poverty provides a breeding ground for terrorism" (*New York Times* 9/11/02).

Israeli—but rather at specific actions taken by specific governments.[11] In spite of this, the American audience willing to listen to reasoned analyses is just too small, the dissemination of disinformation so egregious as to be overwhelming, and the political rewards of mass ignorance too stunningly attractive for this to be widely understood in the United States.

It hardly seems germane to debate yet again the proper term for describing the phenomenon known variously as *Intégrisme*, political Islam, fundamentalism, Islamicism, radicalism, et cetera. Nor does it seem compelling to attribute its origins solely to the failure of development ideology, or disenchantment with growth policies, or even merely to an abstraction like postmodernity. I would insist that harsh or "retrograde" Islamicist social movements are profoundly context-specific, and that they are therefore the result of many social factors. Further, what has been ignored for far too long is that "not all of the contemporary movements in religion, even if they aim at superseding modernity, have as a short-term aim seizure of power and revolutionary transformation of society... Many have adopted the most sophisticated techniques of modernity and tried to dissociate them from the secular culture, to show that there is no necessary connection between the two" (Kepel 1994:5).

It would be one thing if the terrorists were drawn from the economically disadvantaged fringe of society. But frequently, they are not usually poor but from the middle class, are materially well off, and are educated enough to be motivated by abstract concepts. Nor are they insane (Sprinzak 2000).

> *Any connection between poverty, education, and terrorism is indirect, complicated, and probably quite weak. Instead of viewing terrorism as a direct response to low market opportunities or lack of education, we suggest it is more accurately viewed as a response to political conditions and long-standing feelings of indignity and frustration (perceived or real) that have little to do with economics*
>
> —Krueger and Maleckova (2002)

---

[11]Or, as in Denmark, the actions of independent media, specifically publishing cartoons which not only depicted a likeness (imagined of course) of the Prophet Mohammed, which is blasphemous, but also explicitly mocked Islam as a religion devoted to violence.

Clearly, political engagement is a more exact measure of an individual's potential to become a terrorist than his or her economic or social status. It is not the poorest who emigrate, or the most downtrodden who riot, or the most exploited who go on strike.

In the manner of Antonio Gramsci's optimism of the will and pessimism of the intellect (Gramsci 1991), I think, despite the gloomy forecasts, there is an historic opportunity before us to understand the relationship between poverty[12] and religious zealotry. If the age of extremes is ever to draw to a close, this opportunity must not be squandered.

I went to Morocco to study Muslims and the politics of faith in an effort to tease out the distinctions between tradition, modernity, and postmodernity. I was curious about what attracts men and women to "retrograde" intolerant ideologies such as that of the Moroccan cleric and polemicist, 'Abd As-Slam Yasine. He is popularly known as the leader of *al-'Adl w-al-Ihsan*, and was under house arrest in Salé, Morocco from 1986 until 1996. He and his followers view the monarchy and political actors representing it as corrupt, and eschew participation in events organized by the state, the better to oppose it (Brand 1998). Why is it that of 400 Moroccan university students surveyed in 1984, 55% felt that "the backwardness of our society is due to our renunciation of the true Islamic religion," while 65% thought that the *Qu'ran*'s teaching should be emphasized "to reconstruct the cultural identity of Moroccans" (Tozy 1984:248–252)?

Clifford Geertz supplied the beginning of an answer when he noted in *Islam Observed* (1971) that contemporary reformist Islam entailed an ideological transformation of orthodoxy. The assurances guaranteed by earlier revelation were no longer secure: religious symbols were changing from being "imagistic revelations of the divine" to becoming "ideological assertions of

---

[12] I conceive of "poverty" not as an absolute status, but rather one that varies depending upon the specificities of a particular place. Thus an African refugee who may die of starvation at any moment is qualitatively different from a Moroccan who cannot afford an automobile.

the divine's importance" (1971:62). Today it is not enough to believe, one must act in order to prove one's faith. In short, agency defines belonging.

How is this accomplished in an era of global capital, mass advertisement campaigns, and the saccharine-sweet appeal of conspicuous consumption amid the boastful crowing of democratic capitalism's new world order? What is happening to individual Muslims as their governments jockey for the favors of wealthy Western economies? What are the effects of shifting capital/labor disputes on daily life in one small corner of the global "playing field"? Are traditional class and status hierarchies changing? If so, how?

Fez, Morocco seemed an excellent place to explore the relationship between religiosity and unemployment/underemployment and the durability of tradition because it is the religious capital of Islam's westward expansion in the seventh century, CE (Common Era). It is also a complex city fraught with the tensions of other quickly expanding metropolises without particularly robust economies. Of special relevance to my research, Fez happens to boast a relatively unchanged (by colonialism) architectural infrastructure, parts of which date from the city's founding in the eighth century. Fez's old city, the medina, is a massive tourist attraction, and deemed so important that it was recently granted the status of World Heritage City by UNESCO. A fund has been established by that body to "save" the old city from the depredations of overpopulation and poverty. This fund is strictly dedicated to restoring architectural features, however, especially those that might attract tourism. The people who live in Fez's ancient city are apparently less interesting to the likes of UNESCO.[13]

I chose to examine these ideas concerning modernity, tradition, faith, agency, and belonging in a specific urban context—a small neighborhood (*huma*) in Fez, Morocco's imperial and spiritual

---

[13]In 1994, 40% of the households in the *Quarawiyyine* quarter of Fez averaged 4–10 people each, and lived in a single room. Nationwide, fully 35% of the urban population lived under "precarious" and "illegal" conditions (Ksikes 1994).

crown jewel. In doing so, I have been forced to confront an interpretation of agency, faith, and modernity as they were presented to me by my friends and informants, an interpretation based not on the divine, but on the profane, the vulgar, and the material. I am speaking of that emergent subject who results from repeated encounters between "ex-primitives" and "postmoderns," the tour guide.

CHAPTER 3

Tour Guides

Delicatus ille est adhuc cui patria dulce est, fortis autem cui omne solum patria est, perfectus vero cui mundus totus exilium est (**The man who finds his homeland sweet is still a tender beginner; he to whom every soil is as his native one is already strong; but he is perfect to whom the entire world is as a foreign land**).

—(THE DIDASCALICON, HUGH, ABBOT OF ST. VICTOR, 12TH CENTURY)

It is so easy to become lost in Fez. Today, there are no end of boys who press their services as guides on the unwilling visitor, follow him at a distance despite his curt refusal and confident waving of the Guide Bleu, *waiting for the moment, and it inevitably comes, when the confused and disoriented traveler turns to him and asks to be led back to the Bou Djeloud {the Blue Gate}.*

—DOUGLAS PORCH (1982:92)

Now, after September 11th and the Iraq wars have firmly established fundamentalist Islam as a replacement for communism as America's preeminent public enemy,[14] Morocco is ardently trying to position itself as a moderate, modern Muslim state. It is banking on its geographically strategic importance to European and American interests because it occupies the Atlantic and Mediterranean littoral of Northwest Africa. It is also counting on its appeal to tourists seeking the pleasures of sun and sand, both of which Morocco has in

---

[14]The construction of Islam as America's enemy has been building since at least 1979 when Iran's Shah Reza Pahlevi was overthrown by supporters of Ayatollah Khomeini.

abundance. Increasingly, tourism has come to be understood as a means to augment national coffers and help repay a crushing debt to the International Monetary Fund and the World Bank.[15] Morocco's annual budget is $19.3 billion (CIA 2008). Currently tourism in Morocco contributes three billion dollars annually to the national economy (Moroccan American Trade and Investment Council 2008). Approximately 47 percent of Morocco's labor force is employed by the service sector (CIA 2008). The employment figures for Morocco's tourism industry are exceedingly incomplete, however. Many who earn their living from tourism are not considered "employed" for they have no officially recognized capacity as tourism industry employees. Nevertheless, these figures are useful for illustrating just how important tourism actually is to the officially measured Moroccan economy.

Tourism, quite simply is the largest industry in the world. It has overtaken petroleum and motor vehicles as the leading export earner in the world (Youell 1998). Taken as an ensemble, passenger transportation, hotels, restaurants, and leisure activities (including those advertised as "cultural"), tourism is expected to account for roughly eight trillion dollars globally in 2008 and rising to roughly $15 trillion over the next ten years according to the World Travel and Tourism Council. This growth in numbers will also reflect changes in the kinds of people who travel and the kinds of experiences they will purchase. One can expect generally older tourists who are likely to spend more money per visit.

According to my observations as well as those of The Economist (3/23/91, p. 42), most tourists visiting Morocco come from five countries: the United States, Germany, the United Kingdom, Japan, and France. Due in part to American deregulation of its airlines, travel over great distances has become less expensive and far more common, thereby facilitating tourism and travel in general. And despite 9/11, its aftermath, a weakening US dollar, and rising fuel costs, the World Travel and Tourism Council notes that regional emerging markets in Africa, Asia Pacific, and the Middle East are experiencing higher growth rates than the world average, at 5.9%, 5.7%, and 5.2% respectively.

Tourists are valuable commodities to the vacation-brokers and tourism industrialists, and this is not lost on the Moroccans of

---

[15]Total external debt as of 2007 is $16.86 billion (CIA 2008).

humble origins who find themselves unable to realize the economic aspirations that the movies, television advertisements, and situation comedies imported from the West ceaselessly encourage. Because of structural changes in Moroccan society, steady population growth, unemployment, and in particular the growth of industrial tourism, those young Moroccan men lucky enough to live in one of the imperial capitol cities famed for their ancient medinas (Fez, Marrakesh, or Meknès), have been, since the late 1970's, increasingly drawn to work for what is perceived to be easy money earned by guiding tourists.

It is important to note that Morocco has been a destination of distinction for European and American elites ever since France gained political control there in 1912. Winston Churchill spoke of the Mamounia hotel in Marrakesh as "the most lovely spot in the whole world" (Humphreys 2003). More recently, often younger American, German, and Japanese travelers eager for an inexpensive good time, risky sex, and easy access to illegal drugs have arrived buoyed by songs like "Marrakesh Express" by Crosby, Stills, Nash, and Young, the legends of Jimi Hendrix relaxing on the beaches South of Essaouira, or the glamorous parade of celebrities who still go to Morocco.[16] They were, for Moroccans, an easy source of fun, money, and an opportunity to escape the rigid confines of class and status, which relegated them to low-paying menial jobs or worse still, chronic unemployment.

Today, in the face of shrinking legitimate opportunities, guiding is understood to provide a measure of autonomy unavailable to any but the upper classes, hence it is attractive to young, ambitious Moroccans, both male and female. Unofficial guides are considered unsavory characters, harassing outsiders and giving Morocco a bad reputation among tourists internationally, thereby being very

---

[16]"Now the drugs and sex are (mostly) gone, film keeps southern Morocco's celeb quotient high. The Atlas Studios, in the tiny one-camel town of Ouarzazate, offers cheap film-making facilities to Hollywood. Costs are a fraction of those in America, and there are 300 clear sunny days a year. So Morocco has in recent years become the exotic backdrop of choice for foreign producers, standing in for Tibet in Martin Scorsese's *Kundun*, Somalia in Ridley Scott's *Black Hawk Down*, and Egypt in the French hit *Astérix and Obelix: Mission Cléopatra*. *Hideous Kinky* with Kate Winslet was also filmed there" (Humphreys 2003).

bad for business. Indeed, this is not unique to Morocco. As Pruitt (1993) has shown, similar attitudes prevail in Jamaica:

> *When those who have been disenfranchised from institutionalized tourism seek direct access to the largesse associated with tourist dollars, they are maligned and persecuted as detriments to the national interest. While the government has failed to provide for the interests of the majority of the society, national leaders continue to admonish citizens to cooperate with the establishment's tourism program for satisfying tourists' desires for a carefree, fun-filled holiday (1993:162).*

My informants were the ones who approached obvious outsiders, tourists, and travelers offering their services as self-styled impresarios of their city's finest cultural artifacts and experiences. Eagerly catering to the Western traveler's desire for illicit pleasure, such as hashish, sex, or alcohol in an "exotic" setting, they were like knights in tailored suits or "*jellabas*" (traditional hooded woolen gowns).

They sought to earn the confidence of tourists in exchange for whatever they could get. They are commonly known as illegal or unofficial guides. They called themselves *geeyad* (guides). I called them the Sharks[17].

I am convinced that where objects of tourists' desire are to be found, tourism itself is having a powerful effect upon the way people, especially the young, conceive of themselves as members of local culture, and upon the long-term nature of local and national economies as these young people come of age in an era of belt-tightening and world economic turbulence. According to MacCannell, the "commercialization of ethnological performance and display co-developed by formerly primitive peoples and the international tourism and entertainment industries, is potentially a long-term economic adaptation" (1992:18). This certainly seems to be the case in Fez, Morocco.

---

[17]When I asked one of my informants what he thought of my term, "the Sharks", he made a face and said that he did not like it at all. "Sharks are stupid animals," he told me, "*geeyad* are neither beasts nor fools." While I agree with this opinion, I still like my term because of the association with ruthlessness and voracious appetites. It also reflects the fear that tourists have of the *geeyad*.

"As people thread their ways through the intricate networks of urban social structure, they choose or forge paths which accommodate their needs, reward their aspirations, and justify their humanity" (Berreman 1972:584). Though this remark was penned in reference to urban India, this too certainly seems to be true in Fez. In light of this, I think that "the guiding way," as one of my informants put it, ought to be understood as a response to the shrinking opportunity structure of contemporary Morocco. Selling experiences to tourists is a form of deviance that is also modifying traditional attitudes and occupations.

The oldest Muslim kingdom, Morocco has long been a classic site for anthropological fieldwork. Yet no work has explicitly concerned itself with the Moroccans many visitors to Morocco would be most likely to meet. Tourists arrive primed by the lustrous enticements of travel magazines touting Morocco as a "world class destination," a "land of forbidden pleasure," and a sensuous escape.[18]

The bulk of my time while in Morocco came to be spent among a group of young men, all of whom had worked or were working as unlicensed tour guides in the city of Fez.[19] Most were still guiding in 1993, six years after I first met them. A few had saved enough money, or had accrued enough support from patrons, to open shops of their own, catering exclusively to tourists. Only two had official licenses to work as guides, and these they had acquired through bribery.

By exploring the guides' fragmented sense of their own power and powerlessness within a context of social and economic change, their search for justice and agency in an unjust world can be understood as a modernizing force dependent upon an illusion of pre-modern authenticity, and as an effort to resist a repressive authoritarian state. In doing so, they cling to Islam as a core feature of their identity. Despite their sybaritic orientation and fast living, they unambiguously identify themselves as Muslim, even as they contradict every normative orientation to Islam.

---

[18]None other than the romance novelist Danielle Hayes wrote about Morocco (1994), "To be in Morocco is to enter the realm of the senses."

[19]I met and interviewed one young woman (19 years of age in 1994) who worked as an unlicensed guide in Fez. Her street name, ironically, was "*al wild*" which means "the boy."

The Sharks are strategically situated at the intersection of modern and "traditional" conventions. They are quintessential marginal men: they are "in" but not "of" both city and village. They know the limits, as well as the virtues, of both. Occupying a liminal position, they have to know enough of the traditional culture to be able to effectively market that tradition to affluent Westerners; and they have to know enough about the affluent West to be good at appealing to tastes honed by the desire for adventure, and the desire to bring back souvenirs of their exotic interlude "outside the passage of time."

The distinction between *geeyad* and official guides bears some scrutiny. The *Office Nationale Marocaine du Tourisme* licenses the latter. They are essentially the embodiment of Morocco's efforts to distance itself from its bad reputation as a dangerous land of unscrupulous barbarians.[20] Licensed guides represent an effort to make Morocco "safe" and welcoming to timid tourists, but, there are those young affluent tourists from Europe, Japan, and the United States who want something more raw, adventurous, and "authentic" than anything the packaged tours and official guides can offer. Hence the market niche for the unlicensed unofficial guides.

As features of the tourist's imagined landscape, like Scylla and Charybdis, Morocco's unofficial guides' reputations precede them worldwide. Guidebooks to Morocco are replete with warnings about the touts and guides of Fez, Marrakech, and Tangiers. The popular guidebook *Let's Go! Spain, Portugal and Morocco* (1991) goes so far as to urge visitors to Fez to hire an official guide to avoid the generalized hassles posed by unofficial guides, and also to bring water and other supplies in case one gets lost in *Fès al-bali*, home to over 200,000 souls. The implication is that unofficial guides are not to be trusted, that they are even dangerous men; that amidst the exotica of a magical medieval (yet modern) Muslim city one is a form of prey.[21] The fact is that the unofficial guides themselves are prey of the Moroccan state: unofficial

---

[20] According to *The New Shorter Oxford English Dictionary*, the term "barbarian" has its origins in Arabic: "Arab *barbar* (berber); barbaria, land of barbarians (an old name for the western part of North Africa)."

[21] Paul Bowles' "A Distant Episode" (1989), though not set in Fez, exploits this fear as fully as possible.

guides are subject to harassment from corrupt police who extract "protection" money, or even impose arrest for the seemingly trivial offense of guiding without a license. Every unofficial guide I came to know in Fez had either already been through the municipal jail, or had been shaken down by the police's *Brigade Touristique*.

As I waited for my flight from New York's JFK airport to Casablanca on Royal Air Maroc, I found myself sitting with fellow travelers in a sterile, windowless lounge, under the drab glow of full fluorescent lighting, and listened as they swapped stories of vacations in the most far-flung corners of the map: Alaska, China, "Rhodesia." They were elderly white men and women each trying to outdo the other couple's tales of sumptuous lodgings, gourmet meals, or spectacular views. After a while I asked if any of them had been to Morocco. "Yes," said several couples, "but we'll not go back." I heard this sentiment expressed repeatedly in Morocco as well as elsewhere and it was corroborated by friends who travel a great deal more than I do. When I asked why this might be so, I found a non-specific dissatisfaction to be rather common among tourists returning from Morocco. This was often attributable to what tourists and others describe as personality conflicts with specific Moroccans, and/or the perception of a general expression of resentment on the part of Moroccans toward the outsider.

In an effort to explain this common impression of veiled malevolence, I wish to avoid the abstractions that are alluded to by Entelis (1989) who attributes a certain truculence to "the Moroccan personality." Others are more precise, but the focus is on European representations of Moroccans in Europe (Alloula 1988, Mansouri 1988). Visitors to Morocco may arrive with all sorts of preconceptions, the expectations hyped by romanticized tourist brochures, et cetera, as well as the accreted layers of orientalist[22] residue. Yet this alone is rarely sufficient to account for such widespread reports of unpleasant results from intercourse (sexual or not) with real Moroccans. I prefer a more materialist explanation, one which may be applicable to a wide variety of situations in which bargaining occurs. Specifically, the economist Ellingson suggests that

---

[22] Following Said (1978), I understand "orientalism" to mean an essentialized realm originally separate from and unsullied by the West, one that has no Cartesian order to it, except that which is imposed by colonialism.

> *{w}hen the pie's size is certain, evolution favors the 'fair' strategy; accept any share greater than or equal to one half, reject any smaller share. The unique outcome is hence an equal split. In noisy environments, more flexible behavior tends to appear in equilibrium.* Since flexibility attracts greediness, there is then a positive probability of conflict *(1997:581 emphasis added)*.

Conflict in this case arises because the tourist and the Moroccan/guide are frequently each trying to extract maximum advantage in the context of bargaining for services and/or souvenirs.

Unofficial guides are blamed for all sorts of social ills, from petty thievery to prostitution and gambling. I know of no unofficial guide who has committed outright theft—especially from a tourist, nor did I ever find evidence of the guides I knew being involved with gambling operations or prostitution (Rabinow 1977:68–69), though I suspect such activities do occur. A system of informal codes loosely defines the limits within which the *geeyad* operate.

There is honor among guides. One guide will not muscle in on another's "mark" or client, although they may change horses in mid-stream if one has a better relationship with a vendor of products the mark seems interested in—or, for that matter, to maximize any number of advantages one guide might have over another. But this is a negotiation: there is always a bottom line in terms of the percentage of profit made from sales to the mark, and how that money is divided among all who aided in the sales effort. There is also a hierarchy of marks, but "counting coup" as it were on other guides is irrelevant except in terms of bragging rights over how much a foolish tourist paid for this or that, or over how subtle (and not so subtle) insults were delivered to the tourist. In general, the guides I met preferred clients in their mid-twenties to mid-thirties. Such marks tend to have more money, and more expensive tastes.

According to the guides themselves, they must maintain scrupulous integrity toward their clients because otherwise they would lose their business. Moreover, since they are not officially employed by a legitimate tourist agency, they are vulnerable in ways that official guides are not. As such, the guides I knew must always protect themselves by being as honest as possible in order to succeed in the dishonest business of selling to tourists.

At the signing of the General Agreement on Tariffs and Trade in Marrakesh in 1994, the unofficial guides of that city were rounded up, loaded onto trucks and busses, and driven fifty miles out of town as part of a clean-up campaign. There they were left to make it back to Marrakesh on their own, so the story went among the unofficial guides of Fez. Currently, the unofficial guides are the objects of police repression, subject to arrest if seen with tourists. If caught and unable to provide evidence of a powerful patron's protection (*rkeeza*), the minimum sentence is generally two months in jail, with longer sentences imposed for recidivism.

Jail is a place all the unofficial guides know or at least know of. An unofficial guide who finds himself behind bars has few options: if he has money or goods other inmates value, such as Nike shoes, he must sell or trade them for protection and for a place to sleep. If he has no money or goods of value to trade he is likely to become a "girlfriend" to a powerful inmate. Trading sex for protection is common in Morocco's jails, according to my informants.

The guides feared jail. *Al habs* (the jail) is invoked to frighten and chastise obstreperous or contentious members of the crew I spent time with and learned from. There is a distinct age-grade hierarchy determining who can threaten whom. Younger members of the crew deferred to older, "wiser" members in all matters, and listened with rapt attention to tales of the jail. The normal rowdiness fades when incarceration and police repression are the topics of discussion. No one makes casual jokes about being "queen bottom" (*hissess*) or the "top man" (*zammel*) in the verbal jousts over sexual ability and submission when suffering in jail is mentioned.

The guides I met were generally nattily attired young men who had been doing this kind of work since they were school children. They usually begin this work when young because it takes time to acquire and retain the often quite sophisticated expressions and vocabularies of various languages. They must be acutely aware of individual psychology in order to quickly size up marks to determine weaknesses and preferences, the better to present the mark with things they will like and feel good about buying. One of my primary informants, whom I will call Al Malik ("the King"), understands this all too well when he asserts that above all, he "sells words."

The guides size up the mark by virtue of their outgoing gregariousness (an essential personality characteristic of any aspiring guide) and try to inspire enough confidence in them that the mark is willing to be led into the labyrinth of *Fès al-bali*. This is difficult to do, given the reputation of Fez's guides and the hyper-exoticism employed to attract tourists to Fez. Even the best of guides will hedge when asked direct questions about how they go about this crucial phase of what I call "the snag." Once successful, the guide will learn the mark's tastes through conversation and acute observation during the course of a whirlwind tour through the medina. They often concentrate on only a few of the most famous sites followed by picturesque or titillating orientalist set-pieces, such as a narrow alley, or a crowded *souk* (market). From these brief situational tests the guide is often able to quite accurately judge the mark's desires, expressed and unexpressed. One guide went so far as to tell me the colors preferred by various tourist nationalities: Americans, for example, are said to like stripes.

A tourist, or group of tourists, is unlikely to venture very far into the medina without a guide. Those who do happen to wander in will soon find themselves attached to a guide. Even when no such service is requested, and even if nothing is purchased, the guide will tag along doing his best to disorient and confuse the tourist (all under the guise of being helpful), ultimately demanding some money. The game often gets very tense for the tourist who is unused to such in-your-face petty harassment, especially since this is their "holiday." When, on occasion, the tourist becomes exasperated, guides have been known to begin leveling accusations of racism ("You won't hire me because you don't like Arabs!"). This tactic is sometimes effective, resulting in "the snag," or even a handful of change hastily given, just to be rid of the irritating guide and escape the uncomfortable situation.

It is important to distinguish between guides and merchants. The latter are the avowed masters of the deal, the former are like their lieutenants—but with plenty of autonomy to arrange deals of their own for services rendered. Merchants and guides rely upon each other. The merchant greets the mark, makes the mark relax and feel "the genuine warmth of Moroccan hospitality," usually in whatever language the mark is most comfortable with. The successful merchants are the ones who feign disinterest in sales. They repeat to each mark, "It costs nothing to look..." and proceed to show products they suspect the mark will want, usually based upon the guide's insight, gleaned over the course of the tour. They are very good at creating the necessary atmosphere of trust required for the best of cons. For, when the mark feels comfortable, whatever price they pay will seem like a bargain to them: they are indeed buying words.

An example from a fellow traveler's journal helps illustrate the idea:

> "Left Vanessa in a multistory carpark and got a hydrofoil to Tangiers. Although I was expecting them, we were quite scared as we left the boat, by the number of 'unofficial guides' or hustlers which approached us with offers to show us around the city. They directed (attempted to) in all different directions although fortunately we were able to find the train station by ourselves. Much to our disappointment the train did not leave till late in the afternoon, forcing us to spend a day in Tangiers which we definitely did not want to do. Given the problems with the hustlers, we headed to the taxis and got one to the tourist office. This was our first rip off. Having agree {sic} to 4 dirhams, the driver asked for 40 when we arrived—fortunately 40 dirhams is only $5. We hired an official guide who showed us the sights before taking us to a rug shop where we got mint tea and a high pressure sales spiel. Much to my surprise we ended up buying a rug. Our most expensive souvenir yet—$200 for a medium sized Persian rug. We left the store in shock that we'd actually bought one and continued around the medina—the main market area of the old town, full of merchants—fruit, vegetables, meat and spices. Then we experienced a traditional Moroccan meal and were ripped off a second time (or 3rd if you include the rug purchase). Our guide ordered for us and we quite enjoyed the meal until the bill came. We paid ten times what the meal should have cost—our own fault for not being vigilant. Our guide certainly did well on the commissions. We returned to the train station to wait for our train—cowering near the other backpackers for comfort to avoid all the other hustlers. While we waited for the train we met Sam, a French student, originally from Morocco who could speak Arabic, and Duncan, a young solo traveler from England who had just bought 2 things he really didn't want. (In the same way that we had bought the rug.)

> Duncan lost his Eurail Pass in the made {sic} rush to get on the train but got it back thanks to Sam who had a few words to the train conductor when he came by. We arrived at Meknes long after dark and were pleased to tag along with some French students who helped us find cheap accommodations—$12 (100 dirham) for a double and a single bed in one room which we shared with Duncan"
>
> —ANONYMOUS (1994)

Tourists are not alone in feeling betrayed. The guides too are accustomed to the petty betrayals that are inflicted by tourists. In the real world, if a relationship is established there is usually a reciprocal obligation involved, if only implicitly. But in the ersatz Morocco, one pays and then leaves. No relationship exists beyond the transaction. In the real Morocco, one leaves and then pays. In other words, a connection has been established and honor requires that one maintain it. Tourists rarely grasp this feature of social life in Morocco, regardless of how much they may profess to be intoxicated by Moroccan hospitality, generosity, and warmth. Rarer still are those who keep their end of the bargain. For example the guides have heard countless promises to send them copies of photographs, or cassettes, or compact discs, or any number of items that might establish genuine sociability. So few such promises are kept that it is not surprising that the guides are fatalistic and cynical not just about tourists, but about most everything. Several examples from my journal illustrate this.

> Morocco's soccer team made the World Cup playoffs hosted by the United States in 1993. The city was abuzz with excitement, men and boys played soccer with more than the usual intensity. Morocco was scheduled to play Saudi Arabia for a chance to enter the semi-finals and face Germany. There was a raucous party in anticipation that evening at Al Malik's shop. As the kickoff approached, we moved the party down the alley to another much more sumptuous carpet bazaar where there was a television. We rolled out beautiful kilims and stretched out to enjoy the American coverage of the game in luxury. The American network aired short tourist-oriented 'background' introductions to each team's country. The introduction to Morocco caused howls of pleasure from those assembled. It relied primarily on abstractions such as sun, sand, mysterious and sensuous veiled women, dark handsome men. There was some discussion among the group about the superficiality of the portrayal. When I asked Al Malik how he felt about Morocco's team playing in the World Cup hosted by the United States, he simply shrugged

and said, 'Even if Morocco could win, it would not be allowed to happen.' Morocco lost to Saudi Arabia.

Also from my journal:

After a long December evening of conversation and camaraderie, I decide not to remain in the old city to sleep; I walk instead back to my bed in the apartment I have rented in the Ville Nouvelle *about three miles away. The gates of each* huma *used to close at nine or ten in the evening (no one seems quite sure), and the main gates of the medina used to close as well. Some parts of the city still do close. For example, the streets leading to the densest part of the old city, the* souks *of the* kissaria, *are blocked every night except during the first nights of* Ramadan, *when hordes of young men and boys light firecrackers and small explosives in celebration. But as one friend told me, the primary motive is to frighten their sisters and mothers, and to annoy their uncles and fathers. Such mayhem is still several months away, and the neighborhood's gates remain open.*

Chill winds whip through the medina's narrow cobblestone streets at this hour, some time between midnight and four in the morning. I don't know the exact time, having loaned my wristwatch to one of the guides. He asked to borrow it because material goods from beyond Morocco, especially stazen *(the contracted form of the French noun* les États-Unis), *lend the possessor great status—no matter that my watch has a Japanese-made movement and a dial made in Taiwan. No one but drunkards, 'bad men with knives' (so my friends warn me), and I are out so late at night, and in this cold. The drunks,* meskine *(a catch-all term for unfortunates), are huddled in doorways, bundled in rags, gibbering. The so-called knife fighters lean on corners here and there, staring from beneath their knit caps at everything that moves. I walk steadily, meeting any gaze defiantly from beneath my own knit cap, the sound of my steps echoing like small-caliber pistol shots on the cobblestones. "Get me out of here," I think to myself. But at the same time, I want to be here; for it is at such an unlikely hour that the city streets are most easily navigated and, contrary to popular opinion, quite safe.*

One can best appreciate the funnel-like spider web that is Fez at night, orange light from sodium-arc street lamps playing crazily across the slanting stone walls, reflecting off of tile rooftops, and casting shadows that shroud the way in uncertainty. Smells guide me: the bitter acrid scent of strong chemicals used to mask fouler, septic system odors suggests an older, poorer family's home; rotting vegetation means the markets of Funduk Yehudi; while the fishmonger's familiar rankness means I've come nearer the Mellah, *and thus will soon break through the walls into the open of the Boulevard Moulay Youssef leading to the* Ville Nouvelle. *From there it is a straight shot along the wide, well-lit sidewalks of the* Ville Nouvelle *to the Avenue des Sports, and then across to the train station, and finally up to my street.*

The apartment I have rented is in a building in a newer section of the Ville Nouvelle. *Like other modern buildings owned and inhabited by wealthier Moroccans, mine has a night watchman. His name is Ahmed. He has a curious 'command post' from which he surveys the ebb and flow of traffic on the street throughout the night. It is a large cardboard box out of which he has fashioned an all-purpose foxhole. He has a small shelf in front with a hole cut out to hold his glass of very sweet and viscous coffee-flavored milk. He keeps a small transistor radio down below the shelf. His seat is a purloined school chair that he covers with a worn sheepskin. The lines on his face are deep. He smokes strong cigarettes of Moroccan manufacture, 'Casa Sports.' One night I asked to try one. He refused to let me, and in response to my repeated entreaties said only,* 'Kmi Casa Sports; li 'l kaboor' *(Smoke Casa Sports; go to the cemetery). He leaves around sunrise each morning. Ahmed the night watchman and I exchange a few words about the frigid night. Each time I come home late at night Ahmed teaches me a new phrase and quizzes me about the last one. This time it's* 'Allah y saub' *(Allah makes it so), referring to the fatalistic attitude toward physical deformity: they are that way because Allah willed it to be thus. Period. A comforting way of dealing with adversity, for it attributes specialness by the grace of Allah to what others might be tempted to see as misfortune.*

Early in the Spring Ahmed was replaced by a younger, more taciturn man. He told me, after I had inquired as to Ahmed's absence upon returning from the medina late one night, that Ahmed had fallen gravely ill from too many nights out in the cold. Ahmed died later that year.

All of my informants entertained fantasies of escaping from Fez. They envisioned themselves eventually finding and marrying a European. Although the full implications of this are rarely confronted, it remains a powerful fantasy. They did not see guiding as a way of life, rather it is a way of postponing the responsibility of adulthood while living well, and being able thereby to enjoy—at least partially—the leisure they see tourists as having. Consumption is therefore a basic component of their worldview. Leisure is to be consumed, replenished by some kind of minimal "work," and then consumed again. The cycle repeats itself *ad infinitum*. In short, leisure is earned and then used as a marker of success. "Making it" means being able to have other people work for you.

In this sense, my primary informant, Al Malik, has made it. He owns a modest carpet shop and controls the labor of a pair of blanket weavers. He also has three young men working for him: Sidi Zitoun, age 31, is a gifted salesman, fluent in French and confident in English, Spanish, and German; Tattoo, age 20 is his apprentice; and Muscles, age 18 is the gopher and general assistant. They sell blankets woven on the premises, and several kinds of carpets, (*Hanbel, Kilim* and *Zarbia*[23]). But, primarily, regardless of the object or experience on offer, words are ultimately the merchandise. Of the approximately 1000 unofficial guides in Fez, a loosely knit group of twenty regularly brings customers to Al Malik's shop where, it is hoped, the words will entice the tourists to buy. The "selling words" have their desired effect often not only because they are indeed mellifluous, but also because of the context in which they are uttered.

Fez itself is seemingly chaotic to an outsider. There is no Cartesian order to the old city (*Fès al-bali* or simply the medina), in marked contrast to the new city (*Fès Ville Nouvelle*) built roughly one mile from the medina's walls by the French in the early decades of the twentieth century. *Fès al-bali* is downright bizarre: a walled city of roughly 200,000 souls wherein no cars can pass, for the widest cobblestone "streets" are perhaps four meters across at their least constricted points. Most alleys are no broader than one's shoulders and two passersby must turn sideways in order to slip past each other. The medina is a canyon land of perpetual shadows, the narrow, twisting passages between structures always cool, except for the quarter hour at high noon when the Sun's light shines directly overhead.

---

[23]*Kilim* is a word of Turkish origin that refers to a pileless textile for a variety of uses. They are produced by one of several flatweaving techniques that have a common or closely related heritage and are practiced in the geographical area that includes parts of Turkey (Anatolia and Thrace), North Africa, the Balkans, the Caucasus, Iran, Afghanistan, Pakistan, Central Asia, and China (Hull, Luczyc-Wyhowska, and Barnard 2000). *Zarbia* literally means "carpet"; the guides used it to refer to any carpet that is not a *kilim. Hanbel* is the term the guides use to refer to blankets.

It is among these *ruelles* that the guides ply their trade, for "hidden" from outsiders are the "secret charms" of this marvelous jewel of a city, to borrow the vocabulary of exoticism. Even armed with the best of the guide books available, however,[24] Fez's old city is so strange to an outsider that a guide can be most welcome, doubly so if he or she can be of use in repelling what tourists and other outsiders perceive to be the ceaseless harassment by zealous hustlers hawking goods and services. In fact, one of the guides' primary functions is to protect their clients while reaping profit for themselves in the demimonde of rapacious merchants and hustlers that inhabit this fascinating metropolis.

---

[24] The *Office Nationale Marocaine du Tourisme*'s colorful-yet-vague impressionistic maps marked with the main points of interest cartooned onto the tracery of city streets are useful only to mark one as an outsider and, as such, fair game for the hustlers. There is not an accurate map of Fez available to the public. Even the best maps ignore the smaller capillary alleyways; they are simply too small. In a very real sense then, there is no map, only cognitive maps, the fruit of experience.

CHAPTER 4

Finding Fez

> *Men are becoming effeminate and address each other as 'Your Lordship'; in Africa where cancer reigns there are, besides the Amazons, houses of prostitution for effeminate males in both Fez and Morocco, and there are a thousand other filthy practices as well.*
>
> —Tommaso Campanella (1623)

> *Many loathed the town on sight. The austere charm of Fez seen from a distance began to diminish as one approached the gates, riding slowly past mounds of putrefying animal carcasses. One then plunged into a maze of narrow streets and cul-de-sacs of such complexity that, without a guide, a European almost never reemerged.*
>
> —Douglas Porch (1982:49)

My interest in Morocco was initially inspired by Paul Rabinow's *Reflections on Fieldwork in Morocco* (1977). Like him, I was transfixed by the ebb and flow of repartee in the public places of *mudun maghrebi* (North African walled cities). But, unlike Rabinow, I wanted to experience life in a city, not a village. What better, more challenging place than Fez to seek such interaction?

"Fez," as Paul Bowles puts it, "is the place where nothing is direct. Going into the Medina is not like entering a city: it is more like becoming a participant in a situation whose meaning is withheld. There is a sense of deviousness and accompanying intrigue in the air, and the inhabitants do little to mitigate this impression" (1991:3).

The city of Fez has long had an evil reputation despite its architectural masterpieces and spiritual gravitas. Perhaps this has to do with its lack of Cartesian precision. Or, maybe, its introspective architecture. My hunch is that Fez enjoys such a bad and dangerous reputation because it is, or rather was, so modern, opulent, and successful in its day—from the 12th century CE to the early 20th century, and the beginning of French colonial rule.

According to the Moroccan historian, Dr. Mohamed Mezzine, while the history of Fez dates to its founding in the 8th century, the city's rise to prominence began with the collapse of the Almohad dynasty and its replacement by the Merinides' own dynasty in the 13th century. Under the Merinides, Fez flourished and became the regional entrepôt for all significant commercial activity, controlling trade along the East-West and the North-South axes. The Merinides commissioned mosques, religious schools (*medersa*), public fountains, *Fez J'did* (an administrative *quartier*), and magnificent palaces (Le Tourneau 1961). The efflorescence of the arts under Merinide patronage has made Fez the tourist attraction it currently is. Capitalizing on UNESCO's designation of Fez as a World Heritage City, the *Office Nationale Marocaine du Tourisme* is aggressively marketing Fez as a product for international consumption. Its descriptions make maximum use of the idea of exoticism.

> *The Holy City of Fez is a jewel of Spanish-Arabic civilization. Fez does not reveal its secrets easily. Secretive, shadowy, they need to be discovered little by little, with reverence. Only in this way can the splendours of Medersa architecture be fully appreciated. Only in this way will the call of the medina temt {sic} you. Bustling with artisans and merchants, its captivating sounds, fragrances and colours mesmerise the visitor with a constant swirl of activity* (Office Nationale Marocaine du Tourisme 2000).

And:

> *Poetic, particularly at sunrise or sunset, the tour of Fez takes the visitor to another world. With splendid views over the rooftops of the holy town, and sites, rich in history, you will often find yourself plunged in contemplation ...* (Office Nationale Marocaine du Tourisme 2000).

Tempted, mesmerized, and curious the first time I visited Morocco, I went to Fez in late January of 1987. The city was fascinating as a locus of tension between the village and the cosmopolitan world of urbane sophistication. Each neighborhood within the city's walls has a distinctive quality to it making it different from others either because of the work that goes on there (the carpenters' neighborhood, the tanners' neighborhood, the potters' neighborhood, et cetera), or because of who lives there (the Jewish quarter, the Andalusian quarter, et cetera).

An American I had met in Cairo some months before, I will call him Arthur, insisted that when I got to Fez I must look up his friends who would "take care of me." He began to draw a most curious map so that I might find his friend without being dissuaded, or misled by some other Moroccan with designs on my wallet. Arthur's map was replete with such astonishing points of reference as "kid selling cigarettes," or simply, "turn right at the old man." I asked Arthur how he had come to find his friends in Fez.

As he related it to me, Arthur was a peripatetic character who had found himself in Fez, Morocco sometime in 1985 and had met a guide who had introduced him to the ambitious, hard-living young entrepreneur whom I have called Al Malik. Al Malik had just opened his own carpet shop and relied upon the guides to Fez al-bali to bring in much of his business since the space he rented was deep within the old city, effectively hidden from all but the most adventuresome visitors to the medina. Al Malik relied also upon Fez's tradition of patron-client networks to build his business: if he was good to guides, guides would be good to him. During the early 1980's tourism was beginning to boom as an industry in Fez, and had become lucrative not only for the operators of package tours, but also smaller entrepreneurs who catered to the more independent, non-conformist, self-described "travelers" as distinct from "tourists." Generally young or of youthful attitude, these visitors came in search of good times as well as good deals on local handicrafts. Authenticity of experience dominated their search for self among the exotic others of their orientalist fantasy.

Arthur was one such traveler looking for strong hashish and authentic experiences of the exotic Moroccan "other." He and Al Malik got along famously, and Al Malik eventually invited Arthur to stay with him at his family's home in the medina, not far from his shop. Arthur accepted the offer and lived with Al Malik, his mother, brother, and sister for eight months. He learned Moroccan Arabic and the tourist carpet trade, and came to generally enjoy the pace of life inside the medina's walls. Things eventually soured between Arthur and Al Malik, and Arthur decided to leave. I met him after he had been away from Fez for several years, working and traveling throughout the Middle East.

Armed with Arthur's hand-drawn map, I embarked on my search for Al Malik's shop and what became the beginning of my field research. I stepped out of a taxi at the plaza of the Blue Gate, *Bab Bou Jeloud*,[25] where the trail to Al Malik began. The plaza itself is roughly the shape of an isosceles triangle, sloping downward toward the Blue Gate at its apex.

From the outset it was clear that Arthur's map drastically understated the complexity of Fez's labyrinth. At that time, Bab Bou Jeloud was not only the main tourist entrance to Fez's medina and neighborhood of cheap tourist hotels and cafés, but also the central bus station for long-distance connections throughout Morocco. A new bus station has been built since then, far from *Bab Bou Jeloud*, changing considerably the character of this part of town and also making it harder for the guides to snag tourists. But at that time at least five different bus companies used the garages and terminals at the Blue Gate. For every departing coach a gang of touts shouted the destination their bus was bound for, although they were never clear about precise departure times. "*Mazel, mazel*" (not yet), or "*Assabar nisrani*" (patience, Christian) was about as much of an answer one not conversant in Moroccan Arabic was likely to get. The touts often competed with one another to see who could shout the loudest, and each had distinct calls for every destination. Added to the general cacophony was the deep rumbling of buses themselves idling or roaring to life, in either case spewing their pungent exhaust. City buses too would careen past at irregular intervals, honking at the swarms of red Fiat and Peugeot "*petit taxis*" picking up or disgorging passengers.

---

[25]Literally, the "gate of the father of hides [or leathers]." It is an ironic icon for the city, a tourist destination and point of embarkation affording a convenient photo opportunity: the gate's archway neatly frames a minaret when viewed from the proper angle on the sidewalk terrace of a café where guides often wait for potential clients. It was built in 1921 by the French specifically to look "traditional" with blue glazed tiles on the outer wall (hence the nickname of "Blue Gate") and green glazed tiles on the inner wall.

A jumble of open-air markets were also loosely scattered around the triangular sloping plaza within the city walls at the Blue Gate, but not inside the medina proper. This was *al jutaya*, the flea market, where one could find everything for daily or occasional use: used clothing, car parts, farm implements, antique bric-a-brac, shoes, hardware, house wares, a small vegetable market, and an army of mobile snack carts catering to the throngs by selling fresh-squeezed orange juice by the glass, yogurt, chocolate, biscuits and cookies, boiled eggs, mint tea, etc. Families would construct sunshades out of bed-frames and plastic sheets and display their wares as neatly as they possibly could. Elderly women would squat before a small display of items for sale: underwear, shoes, batteries, or a few tangerines. Squadrons of young boys hawking trinkets and souvenirs of Fez plied the crowds of customers of both sexes, who were picking through the treasure: plastic bead necklaces, gold brocade belts for women's gowns, votive candles from the shrine of Moulay Idriss, or a wide variety of European-style, individually wrapped candies. Another character who caught my eye was a man dressed in bright colors, wearing a conical hat with red tassels and small mirrors. He had a goatskin bag draped over his shoulders and brass cups hanging from another belt, like a bandoleer: a water seller, decanting one or two gulps at a time.

Around the edges of the plaza's higher end were parked cars and trucks, guarded by sullen men to whom one paid a few coins for their vigilance. Lower down, closer to the Blue Gate were several cafés lining the sides of the plaza. These were filled with young men, often smoking hashish, playing pinball or cards while lazily watching soccer matches, MTV, or karate adventure-thrillers on the omnipresent television screen. These cafés are the haunts of the unlicensed tourist guides. Thus, not without some trepidation, I climbed out of the taxi and into the tumult and the shouting of hustlers, shoppers, housemaids, travelers, tourists, and beggars. Trailing a stream of curious and insistent would-be guides, I made my way into the medina with the help of Arthur's map. Within half an hour I found Arthur's old friend, Al Malik.

I considered myself a "traveler" and not a mere tourist at the time I met Al Malik, a distinction more apparent than real. Tourists seemed to want to stick to what was familiar without risking physical or emotional discomfort. They were on holiday after all.

Travelers seem to think of themselves as made of sterner stuff, hardier, more adventuresome, and specifically interested in their experiences interacting with the "other," although this often means other travelers, not locals.

It is precisely to those such as myself during my first visit to Fez in 1987, that Al Malik and his network appeal so strongly. They offer the exotic experience of personal contact with a foreign culture beyond mere cuisine or artifact or guided tour of this or that. They offer camaraderie, fun times, an adventure round every corner, for they are locals ostensibly willing to share their world with the outsider. Or at least that is the perception they project for the outsider's benefit, and their own financial gain.

Having thoroughly enjoyed myself in Fez over the course of a week with Al Malik and his associates, I eventually bought a carpet from him. I paid more than it was worth for it but did not really mind too much because I had had such a fine time with him and his merry bunch. While with them I felt secure, sure that I was not likely to be subjected to "the pushing," the high-pressure sales tactics commonly resorted to when a tourist/outsider is not immediately interested in whatever transaction has been proposed. They acted as protectors, insulating me from the rapacious interests of those who would otherwise take advantage of me, or so I was led to believe. Meeting other guides with Al Malik's introduction made all the difference because it helped to mitigate my outsider's status, allowing the other guides to understand that while they were free to try and do business with me, I had the authority of Al Malik behind me. To treat me poorly or unfairly was in some small measure to disrespect Al Malik. Just as Arthur's introduction to Al Malik made me different from other tourists, Al Malik's authority made me even more different from other tourists. Or so I thought. As a result, I trusted Al Malik. Trust is the con's currency.

Upon my return to Fez six years later in 1993, I went looking for Al Malik. After several forays into the medina, and despite some difficulty remembering the neighborhood's twisting alleyways, I finally found him ensconced in a new shop not far from the old one. He immediately remembered me as Arthur's friend. We reminded each other of good times past and re-cemented our friendship. Eventually, Al Malik was to become one of my primary informants.

CHAPTER 5

Failure Considered and Reconsidered

He said, 'You don't understand, ... there are politics involved here.' I did understand, all too well, I fear. But that understanding was only budding then, it had not taken the form of a story, of a structure that has its own necessity, of an understandable process. It was personal. It was not about politics, it was about me. I was the one left out in the cold.

—Durrenberger AND EREM (1998:25)

Now Hatim sighed, resigning himself to a venture without ending, for it seemed that the longer he chased the answers, the more numerous grew the riddles.

—BUSHNAQ (1986:97)

Conspicuously missing from anthropological literature is a frank discussion of failure.[26] What about all the times that anthropologists do not manage to obtain the data they have sought or to achieve Weberian *verstehen*? Was it merely wasted effort and time? I am persuaded that time in "the field" is never fruitless. It may not produce the desired outcomes (access, data, trust) but there is always at least some small insight gained. I was uniquely privileged to earn a welcomed, if impermanent, place among a group of "notorious" or perhaps "famous" unofficial guides who worked in Fez's medina. Based upon the relationship I had established with Al Malik, and upon other contacts to whom he subsequently introduced me, I was

---

[26]Notable exceptions include Briggs (1970), Durrenberger and Erem (1998), and Kent (1992).

able to learn much about their shared worldview, one often in sharp contrast to the widespread conventional assumptions about them and their work. I also learned of things Al Malik did not want to show me. It is likely that I lost the friendship of men I respected because of mistakes I made while trying to gather information.

As I reflect upon my own experiences in Fez, it would seem that I learned very little of what there is to know. Yet, according to my informants, I was the only *nisrani* ever to speak with them at length about their days, their aspirations, and their fears. What at the time seemed to me to be another lost opportunity, when conversation turned from the daily hustles to the next party, was, now that I look back upon such times, not lost at all. They provided me with the in-group knowledge which brought me the rapport that made my research possible. For example, I learned how to distinguish tourist hashish from the better grades (not too light, nor too black and tarry). I learned how to make a proper hashish cigarette. I learned to navigate the cobblestone alleys of Fez in broad daylight or late at night, despite an evening of red wine, tobacco, and hashish. Even when I failed to learn a new method for selling a carpet or managing an encounter, I had at least tried, and in so doing succeeded in some small way in strengthening my tenuous relationship to, and my own sense of belonging among, people continuously suspicious of the intentions of one another, let alone outsiders from America. Failure then, like authenticity, is relative. As with so much else in human affairs, context determines the meaning of actions, or in this case, knowledge. Such a conclusion is perhaps trivial or banal, but to me it made all the difference in the world.

The practice of anthropology is fraught with ambiguity and tension because people have interests that are threatened or enhanced by what an outsider—with the power relative autonomy confers—is allowed to know or prevented from knowing about them. My familiarity with the details of the unofficial guides' life-worlds could harm those who were my teachers, and this knowledge makes me very uneasy and worried for their well being. Consequently, it has been extremely difficult to write about my experiences among the Moroccans who taught me what I wanted, even needed, to know while not betraying their confidence.

Many versions of my story circulated among them. One held that I was a spy working for a nefarious publisher of tourist guidebooks.

Another maintained that I was conducting unethical research of unspecified description, which led me to be ejected from Morocco for further unspecified reasons of improper conduct. Neither of these versions is "true," but the truth, like authenticity, is a fluid notion, is relative. On one hand, I am not a spy, nor was I engaged in unethical research (I scrupulously adhered to the American Anthropological Association's Principles of Professional Responsibility and the University of California's rigorous Guidelines for the Protection of Human Subjects). Yet, on the other hand, perhaps by the very nature of being an anthropologist I was in a sense spying on people,[27] learning their secrets not even for, from my informants' perspective, a "practical" purpose such as to trade that knowledge for something of value.[28] It is conceivable that my research could in some way be regarded as ethically suspect, for I consorted with people who survived by their wits, manipulating people and contexts, even to deceive them in ways costly to them. They broke laws, they sought my help in doing so, and they used me to legitimate scenarios so as to consummate transactions. All of this could be read as unethical activity.

In my defense and that of anthropological research at large, I must cite the long tradition in American social science of studying deviant behavior so as to explain it in emic terms, from the inside as it were, thereby translating the initially incomprehensibly wrong into something intelligible, and with its own rationality in the context of its occurrence. Anthropologists study practices and beliefs not to justify or condone them, but to explain why and how they exist. This is not to make excuses for dangerous or harmful behavior. It is offered rather in the hope of explaining why people do what they do so as to help, even in some small way, to change the structural imperatives that constrain human potential, and in so doing, contribute to making the world a better, more humane place. This is a vain hope perhaps, but one I nonetheless cannot in good conscience refrain from acting upon. If I erred on the side

---

[27] I wonder if anthropologists are not really spies, if not for states, corporations or individuals, then for science—not an altogether benign enterprise (Broad 1985; Kuletz 1998; Thomas 2001; Tierney 2000).

[28] From my point of view, of course, it was for the eminently practical purpose of advancing scholarly understanding.

of complicity it is because I could find no better method to learn the ways of a specific group of people struggling within the confines of their culture to survive in a world of rapidly changing regimes of reality.[29] With nothing to guide them, these guides made use of whatever was ready-to-hand, like consummate *bricoleurs* piecing together their world one day, and one transaction, at a time.

When I arrived in Fez on the 14th of September in 1993, I naively hoped to study the daily lives of devout Muslim men and women in an effort to understand the relationship between the Moroccan monarchy and Islam in terms of daily household activities and the routines of quotidian behavior with an eye to exploring local kinship networks and their role in immigration to Europe. Nine months later, on May 2nd, 1994 the assistant to the Fulbright Commissioner informed me that Morocco's Ministry of the Interior had not approved my original research project. During the intervening months I had nonetheless managed to learn a good deal about the daily lives of young Muslim men (and one woman) who work for tourists as guides, impresarios, and hustlers. I had in fact decided to expand my focus to include them as well. In response to the Ministry's dictum, I now made of this my entire research project. Fully aware of this new focus of my research, the Fulbright Commissioner assured me that the Ministry of the Interior's decision regarding my initial research proposal was irrelevant since I had not been pursuing it—nor did I plan to pursue the project that had been disapproved. The Commissioner then asked me to submit a revised research proposal reflecting my reorientation so that he could process my request for the two-month extension of funds that I felt I needed to wrap up my work with the guides. This I did one week later. On May 25, 1994 the Fulbright Commissioner telephoned from Rabat to inform me that I was to cease all research activity immediately, and further that the two-month extension of funds granted the previous week was rescinded. In answer to my stunned request for an explanation, he would say only that the Ministry of the Interior was upset that I was still in the country and had requested that I not be granted an extension to continue my research along the "new" line of inquiry. In compliance I stopped visiting my informants and eliciting information from them. I feared

---

[29] In this I am by no means alone. See for example Ferrell and Hamm (1998).

that further contact with them could result in harm to them, for I assumed that my activities were being monitored. This was in fact the case, as I discovered when, before leaving, I met and casually befriended the two undercover police agents who were assigned to me. I then asked one of the guides I knew, whom I had befriended, and whom I met by chance shortly before leaving, to convey my farewells to the others. I dared not visit the latter in person out of concern for their safety. I then left Fez on June 12, 1994, and have not returned since.

As a tale within a tale, my story is framed by what other people thought I was doing. Consequently misunderstanding was a routine feature of my research experiences. I was forced to explain repeatedly that I was not a spy for any organization (although over time I came to have second thoughts about this); that I was working independently; and that I was interested in the guides and industrial tourism in Fez because I wanted to tell the story of tourist consumption of Moroccan culture and how it feeds the local economy. Tourists experience a version of Morocco that Moroccans create for outsiders. Guides contribute by orienting outsiders to culture for sale, which in turn is shaped by Moroccan perceptions of tourists' expectations. It is a complex story, and it is in every respect cultural in Geertz's sense of comprising webs of significance spun by the players themselves (Geertz, 1973). It has aspects of skullduggery: one of my informants murdered his father during the course of my stay in Fez. It has anomalous components: one of the most successful unofficial guides I met is a young woman. It has intrigue: elderly women would often warn the guides of police operations in an effort to help the guides avoid arrest. It has terror: almost all of my informants could count on at least two months in jail each year. It has pathos: informants frequently asked me to write *al haqq* (the truth) so that they could survive the police repression of what they considered to be legitimate entrepreneurship. It has all the passion and joy of satisfaction with a job well done: after a big sale the guides and salespeople involved would relax and spend some of their profits on beer, red wine, whiskey, and hashish, the better to entertain each other with tall tales of the ruses used, the near misses, and the sheer delight of making money by virtue of their wits. My tale of their tales is thus only my version of the experiential raw materials they use to construct and animate the dull interstices of their lives that are, after all, based largely on the whims of tourists' fantasies.

It is difficult to ignore the fact that these words I have fashioned into the stories comprising this account are merely the empty husks of what was once a vibrant tale, animated by the experience of living people, as well as by alcohol and strong hashish. My pallid recreation of their spontaneous outbursts and calculated silences cannot adequately reproduce the power of the words spoken among Al Malik and his *geeyad*.

CHAPTER 6

Meeting My Baker

Say: O you unbelievers,

I do not worship

What you worship,

Nor do you worship

Who I worship,

Nor will I worship

What you worship,

Nor will you worship who I worship:

To you your way,

To me my way.

—THE UNBELIEVERS, AL QUR'AN

In 1993, eight years before Americans were explicitly targeted by enraged xenophobic men who have blamed cultural changes not to their liking on an inherently morally bankrupt—unholy and therefore impure—*jahiliyya*[30] consumer culture, one they understand to be centered in the United States and symbolically represented by

---

[30]Here I am relying upon Qutb's explication of *jahiliyya* as encompassing modern secular systems of political organization, "man's sovereignty over man," which he condemns as being antithetical to Islam. "If we look at the sources and foundations of modern ways of living, it becomes clear that the whole world is steeped in *Jahiliyyah*, (Ignorance of the Divine guidance) and all the marvelous material comforts and high-level inventions do not

the twin towers of what was the World Trade Center in lower Manhattan, I noticed profound anger toward Europeans and Americans among my Moroccan informants in Fez, most of whom were young men like myself—or younger. In conversation after conversation I was told in no uncertain terms that Israel leads America by the nose and that America is ruled by immoral people. The implication was that moral people would act according to principles of justice and compassion, as is any Muslim's duty.

The rhetoric of Christian conservatives (or "Evangelicals,"[31]) within a wealthy capitalist nation declaiming the innocence of civilians in the face of terrorism, the necessity of war to ensure security, and the need for militarily imposed democracy so people can "be free to rule themselves," rang hollow then as now for people like my informants in the old city of Fez, Morocco. In most cases their formal education ended after the equivalent of the eighth grade. Yet they understood, though perhaps not in quite such abstract terms, that the homogenizing effect of global markets is a challenge to cultural uniqueness, and without one's culture, identity quickly fades.

The only thing that seemed to offer a coherent critique of Euro-American hegemony was—and still is for a great many—Islam.

---

diminish this ignorance. This *Jahiliyyah* is based on rebellion against God's sovereignty on earth. It transfers to man one of the greatest attributes of God, namely sovereignty, and makes some men lords over others. It is now not in that simple and primitive form of the ancient *Jahiliyyah*, but takes the form of claiming that the right to create values, to legislate rules of collective behavior, and to choose any way of life rests with men, without regard to what God has prescribed. The result of this rebellion against the authority of God is the oppression of His creatures. Thus the humiliation of the common man under the communist systems and the exploitation of individuals and nations due to greed for wealth and imperialism under the capitalist systems are but a corollary of rebellion against God's authority and the denial of the dignity of man given to him by God" (Qutb 1981:3).

[31] An ABC News poll (18 July 2002) indicated that 83% of Americans identify themselves as Christians, and 37% of Christians define themselves as Evangelical. A Barna Research Ltd. poll (2002) indicated that 61% of all American adults agree that "the Bible is totally accurate in all of its teachings (42% agree strongly, 19% agree somewhat)." Kepel (1994:106) defines fundamentalism as primarily "belief in the *absolute* infallibility of the Bible... especially all the moral or ethical commandments or politico-social injunctions" it contains.

Therefore when the reports began to describe the nineteen hijackers, and their network of accomplices in the hijacking of four airplanes and the subsequent attacks on September 11th of 2001, I was not surprised to learn that some of them were Moroccan. Nor would it surprise me if they came from Fez.[32]

Naïve and unaware of just how suspicious of me many Moroccans whom I encountered really were, I was eager to understand how and why people could be moved to renounce modernity. I thought that by gaining access to the *umma* (community of worshippers) of a "fundamentalist" imam encouraging "retrograde" militant "traditional" Islamic alternatives to the king's compromises, I could begin to search for answers to my questions.

Early in my stay in Fez I had made the acquaintance of a man whom I call Abu Bakr. He was a baker in a café around the corner from a flat I rented in the *Ville Nouvelle* of Fez. I will call it Café Al Akbar. It is a well-known establishment in Fez, not merely for its excellent pastries, but primarily for its reputation as being a place where Islamists work and gather to discuss religious politics. Whenever I hailed a taxi to get home, as I did from time to time, all I had to do was tell the driver to take me to this café. They all knew of it. I was treated to many curious looks in rearview mirrors because of such directions—what would a *nisrani* be doing at café Al Akbar? At the time I had no idea of the political significance of the café, I was simply thrilled to make friends with a Moroccan who might be able to teach me about how Islam was experienced in Fez. Abu Bakr was eager to speak with me, or so it seemed. In fact, what I took to be his friendliness was a zealous desire to bring me into the *umma*, the religious community of which he was a member.

One evening, Abu Bakr invited me to meet his Imam. I agreed, delighted to be invited, and considering this to be an opportunity to begin gathering data on the emic perspective of *Fassie* (of or

---

[32] There are two known Islamist organizations in Fez, *Assirat el Moustaqim* and *Salafia Jihadia*. The former is suspected of involvement in the Casablanca bombings of May 16, 2003. "Moroccan State Prosecutor Mr. Belghiti said [Abdelhaq Moulsabbat]—whom he described as the 'general co-ordinator of the attacks'—was arrested on Monday in Fès." See "Morocco suspect dies in custody" BBC News, 28 May 2003.

pertaining to the city of Fez) piety. Abu Bakr met me at the appointed hour on a warm October evening just after the early evening prayers. He came on a motor scooter. He is a large man, so I was not sure how he expected us both to travel on his groaning mobilette. He smiled and waved to a friend whose name I never learned. He too had a scooter, though he was much slighter than Abu Bakr, and I climbed on behind him. The three of us took off into the dusty, jasmine-scented air of Fez's evening. The streets of the *Ville Nouvelle* were crowded with people going about their business. Their driving was, to my untutored eye, terrifying. We snaked in and out of traffic until we were on the other side of the *Ville Nouvelle*, not far from one of the gates to the old city, or medina.

The scooters were parked and we stepped to a nondescript door and knocked. A password was requested and supplied. We entered and descended a small flight of stairs into a basement room. There I was introduced to several severe-looking young men. There was a rather loud Koranic recitation being played on a tinny stereo. At this time I noticed that I was the only one without a beard. We chatted amiably about Fez for a few minutes while one of the young men went through another door further into the basement rooms. He reemerged eventually and I was led through a room with several large cassette-copying machines, each with a young man busily operating it.

This activity, I later learned, is considered highly suspect by the monarchy. These clandestine operations to copy and disseminate inflammatory anti-monarchy Islamist rhetoric are immediately shut down when they are discovered by the *Sûreté Nationale* (Morocco's state police). I was shown the cases of cassettes ready for shipment. They were recordings of the Imam's speeches.[33]

After admiring their operation, I was taken to a third room where a large man was seated. He looked at me, smiled calmly, and offered me a seat. He asked if I would care for some mint tea. I accepted. He asked one of the young bearded men to fetch it for me, and told the others to leave us. They withdrew and I was face to face

---

[33] I was not able to discover if this operation was associated in any way with either *Assirat el Moustaqim* or *Salafia Jihadia*.

with Abu Bakr's Imam. I will not give his name, for Morocco has imprisoned many religious leaders. We proceeded to discuss trivial topics briefly, until the tea was served. And then, after the young man who brought it had left, the Imam asked me, "Do you believe in God?"

"No, not particularly," I said. "Though I am very curious," I added for I noticed that the Imam began to frown slightly. He saw right through me, though I think he missed the real reason why I had come. We continued to speak of religious matters, the importance of faith, the difficulty of maintaining one's faith in a world of temptations, the necessity for order that religion fulfills in a chaotic and immoral world. He then stopped abruptly, and fixing me with his deep brown eyes, asked why Abu Bakr had brought me to him.

"Because I told him that I was curious about Islam. . ."

". . . and you want to convert?" The Imam finished my sentence with this question, and I was faced with a serious ethical difficulty.

I did not want to convert to Islam. Not being a religious person, I was not interested in becoming a Muslim. Actually, I was interested in what Moroccans thought about the political legitimacy of their king, who claimed descent from the Prophet Mohammed.[34]

But at the time I was somewhat less than willing to share my personal values with this man, and was eager to learn as much as possible from him regarding the society he envisioned for Morocco and beyond. I tried to convey this impression. The Imam became pleasantly detached and made it clear that while he did not really want to speak with me now, he would be happy to discuss theology whenever I felt like it. This was the end of our conversation. I left the building and Abu Bakr's friend gave me a ride back to the bakery.

Abu Bakr avoided me from then on. I made a habit of taking my morning coffee at the bakery (after all it was convenient and they made succulent *pain au chocolat*), but never again received

---

[34]My personal favorite comment regarding Islam and the Alaouite monarch came from a washed up guide. Waving his hashish-laced cigarette and swaggering as he spoke, he told me, "When you see people praying to a donkey it is better to smoke hashish!"

invitations from Abu Bakr or anyone else to participate in religious or political conversations. At first this was frustrating. However, as time passed I began to notice a similar pattern with many of my more respectable, upstanding, and pious acquaintances. After an initially joyful interaction, subsequent encounters became less and less comfortable, if not avoided altogether. With some exceptions, I had failed to gain *entrée*.

I had come to Fez with a preconceived agenda, largely derived from research reports that seemed above reproach. I expected to find that people whose aspirations were blocked would be drawn to a harsh evangelical "retrograde" version of Islam. Though I could not manage to penetrate the oppositional mosques' *umma*, I was able to gain access to a scene in which the people who might have been drawn to the mosque were, instead, drawn to *very nearly* the opposite. The monarchy is hostile to anti-modern Islamicist social movements, so those who were trying to organize and radicalize their *umma* had to be very wary of spies.[35] In a curious way, they were as vulnerable as the Sharks. But the Sharks had to be more open and less risk-averse. Hence, I could gain access to their world, the guiding way.

To put it another way, I went to Fez a structuralist and came out a symbolic interactionist. I began with the expectation that the most disadvantaged members of society would be the most adamantly hostile to the monarchy and the king's version of modernity. Instead, I had to come to terms with resignation, fatalism, and complacency. The structural features of Moroccan society that made my research possible also forced me to consider the ways Structuralism and Symbolic Interactionism require each other. Each, taken alone, distorts and makes it impossible to understand what is going on.

---

[35]One informant, not a guide, insisted in very hushed tones that "one in twenty Moroccans is a paid spy for the king."

CHAPTER 7

Driss, the Weaver

A man who had a monkey wanted to train it to weave at the loom. But even when the man beat it, the monkey refused to learn. One day the man brought one of his sheep to the loom and, while the monkey watched, pretended that he was trying to teach it to weave. The sheep, of course, did nothing but bleat, which made the monkey laugh. The man drew out his knife and said to the sheep, "If you do not learn, I swear by your young lambs that I shall kill you!" The sheep continued to do nothing but bleat. And then the man did kill it. At the sight of the blood, the monkey jumped into the pit of the loom and began to toss the shuttle to and fro as fast as he could go. Hence the saying, "Kill the sheep and the monkey will learn to weave"

—Bushnaq (1986:220)

The presence of Driss, the weaver, elicits a variety of feelings among the tourists who notice him. One is impressed, moved perhaps to pity, by this man at his loom, the rattle of which, as he passes the shuttle through the strings and pushes the pedals to separate them for still another pass, keeps time with the other sounds of the medina. As Sidi Zitoun tells his audiences of potential customers about the "Berber blankets, student blankets, good prices for you my friends, made right here in our shop. . .," Driss keeps weaving, alone or sometimes with Mohammed, an apprentice. For each blanket they get a small percentage, perhaps twenty percent of whatever Sidi Zitoun can wheedle from his customers. Another fifth goes to Sidi Zitoun, and another to the guide and Al Malik pockets the rest. When blankets do not sell, Al Malik does what he can for Driss and his apprentice. Driss has a wife and children at home. Few of the others do, and Al Malik feels the responsibility of patronage; Driss is his client and Al Malik must oblige him when times are lean, as they often are since the boom of the eighties has busted.

"Now" in the nineties, still fewer tourists than ever in recent times venture to Morocco, let alone Fez. Fewer adventuresome hippies and travelers come to Morocco. Instead, there is a larger proportion of package tours from America, Europe, and Japan. These groups are mainly composed of people unwilling to challenge themselves beyond the mild titillations of dull impresarios and the sterile thrills of seeing something exotic as if under glass, safely separate from them. In short, there are far fewer exceptions to the standardized homogeneity of "rational" tourism, such as the Japanese newlyweds I saw when I was first in Fez.

When I asked him about this, Driss shrugged and told me that he has only modest needs, that Allah is wise, and that Al Malik will see to it that buyers arrive. As for himself, he and his loom will work. "*Assabar*," he tells me, "patience," as if to imply that all will come to be—or not be—in the fullness of time. I marvel at Driss: his stoicism, his contrition, his passivity, his calm detachment from the raucous hilarity of the guides and their bragging, their drinking, their preoccupation with material symbols of success (Nikes, European girlfriends, English swear words, and familiarity with the latest exploits of celluloid heroes from Hollywood or Hong Kong).

Driss illustrates one aspect of the complicated ways in which a particular traditional Islamic culture produces "purists" and "opportunists." I was unprepared for the ways the intersections between tradition and modernity could be elaborated. Resignation such as Driss's was integrated in the Islamic culture I experienced with the kind of rational opportunistic calculation of Al Malik and the Sharks, every bit as modern as that of Wall Street stock brokerages. Alongside the opportunists and the purists, there was the call of militant Islam.

CHAPTER 8

Righteous Men of God Defying the Power of an Unjust Ruler

"As long as the King {the Alaouite monarch} oppresses me I will smoke hashish!"

—Anonymous Quotation From One of
the Unofficial Guides

Nishan b'hal l'hout ("Straight like a fish"). A common expression in Fez describing someone who is untrustworthy.

Morocco is a kingdom. The monarch, Mohammed VI,[36] like his father Hassan II before him, is both head of state and *amir al-muminin* (Commander of the Faithful). While there has been a parliament since independence in 1954, it is dominated by pro-regime, conservative political parties unwilling to challenge the king's authority to rule. Nor have elections been widely regarded as free and fair. While Morocco enjoys a long tradition of dissent and loyal opposition, "Power is centralized in the monarchy, which sits atop a national political machine. Political parties and unions have little influence in their own right. Rather, they structure interaction among a fragmented elite, most of which benefits from established patterns of machine politics" (Tessler 1985:38).

Two strategies have been of critical importance to the monarchy for maintaining legitimacy and power: religion and repression.

---

[36]Commonly known as "Speedy Mohammed" he is mocked because of his fondness for personal water craft. Sanoussi (1995) has gone so far as to call him "*Sa Majetski,*" a malapropism based upon the French honorific, "*Sa Majesté.*"

First, as *amir al-muminin* the king is responsible for guiding and directing matters pertaining to religion. The state bureaucracy and the *makhzen* (its related patron-client networks) are further legitimized by the *ulama* (the community of religious scholars), adding to the strength and conservative qualities of the political system in particular, and the society as a whole.

Second, violence is never far from the surface of political activity in Morocco. All too common are political abductions, murders, and disappearances. Violations of human rights such as torture, arrests and detention for political reasons, ghastly prison conditions, and heavy censorship have drawn international criticism.

> *Morocco's attempt to overcome the human rights record of Hassan II, under his more liberal minded son, will not be easy. While Hassan II was an adept politician and a player in the international arena, his success at maintaining relative stability in Morocco and his ability to thwart various challenges to his rule must be measured against the cost society was asked to bear for his accomplishments. With regard to observing human rights and instituting democracy, Hassan II moved reluctantly toward both, bowing to international pressure when expedient and ruling with an iron fist when he deemed necessary.*
>
> —CAMPBELL (1999)

Referring to her interview with *L'Opinion* editor Khalid Jamai, there is what Brand describes as '. . .complicity of the political parties and the intellectuals.'

> *Mr. Jamai stated quite frankly, 'the system continues to work because of our complicity and cynicism.' People are afraid to challenge the king, afraid of what might come after him. So they work within the corrupt framework of the 'known' out of resignation or out of fear of the unknown.*
>
> —BRAND (1998:26)

Resistance to the oppression wrought by Morocco's monarchy takes the form of social banditry, as exemplified by the Sharks. Unlicensed guides serve as informal cultural brokers who "take" from tourists in order to "give" material meaning to their lives of privation, both with respect to local elites and international, jet-setting tourists. In order to explain this model of social banditry as resistance, it is important to show the context of urban Moroccan youth's alienation from political processes and power, as well as their sharply restricted possibilities for social mobility. Powerless and self destructive in political terms,[37] my informants were nevertheless undaunted. They projected a coherent vision of the present for themselves not only in their imaginations, but in their stories and actions on the level of daily practices in relation to their clients. The future was regarded with a fatalistic shrug.

I conceive of the guides as agents bound by both the structural constraints of conformity, and as rebels threatening the normative order. They concentrate on immediate gratification and as such contribute unwittingly to the very forces that oppress them. In this the guides demonstrate an essential difference between themselves and their Islamist neighbors and former classmates. In Morocco, "[t]he organizers of the Islamicist movement are for the most part graduates of the public schools" (Tozy 1993:112). Whereas the guides drop out to pursue temporal material pleasures, the potential recruits for zealotry and *Jihad* fix their desire upon the abstractions of theocracy and paradise.

Daily life in Fez shows how individuals affect what Pierre Bourdieu describes as "structuring structures." According to Bourdieu, the commonsense world of daily life can be described in the abstract in terms of "systems of durable, transposable dispositions, structured structures predisposed to function as structuring structures, that is, as principles of the generation and structuring of practices and representations which can be objectively 'regulated' and 'regular' *without in any way being the product of obedience to rules*" (1972:72; emphasis added). "Structure" for Bourdieu functions here as a verb rather than a noun. The Sharks obey a code of conduct they themselves might not recognize as such. By so doing they contribute to the production and maintenance of social order, even as they act in ways outwardly understood to be disorderly.

Fez's guides are fascinating for their own brand of social banditry, and for the coarse, transgressive lifestyle associated with their mercantile duplicity. Their stock-in-trade is both acceptable and

---

[37] As one guide explained to me, "we kill ourselves by our own hand."

CHAPTER 8: **Righteous Men of God Defying the Power of an Unjust Ruler**

offensive, a form of necessary evil. Someone has to buy the products made by Fez's *artisinat*, the copper artisans, potters, embroiderers, weavers, tailors, tanners, calligraphers, etc. Local producers are beholden to guides for help marketing their wares. But the guides get drunk. They get stoned on hashish before their time,[38] they seek and enjoy illicit sex with clients, they fail to pray throughout the day, and they generally do not attend the mosque on Fridays. I asked what specifically links them to Islam, since this obvious contradiction seemed in need of explanation. The guides I knew unanimously affirmed their identity as Muslims based on their claim that they fast (*sawm*) during Ramadan, the holy month.

While they use sufficient discretion to be able to claim a minimum of dignity before their parents and relevant elders, in the quasi-separate world of guiding tourists and selling souvenirs a more louche persona emerges. A particularly well-executed scam affords an opportunity for a great deal of gloating and derisive pleasure. Guides love to brag and joke among themselves about the exorbitant prices they have succeeded in persuading tourists to pay. I have watched guides laugh in front of clients, boasting in *Dérija* (Moroccan dialect) of their own prowess and the tourist's stupidity. Often they will crow, "I really screwed this or that tourist!" But what to them amounts to a great profit is really only a matter of ten or twenty US dollars, a negligible sum for all but the most hard-bitten budget travelers. However, there are naturally exceptions.

I watched one day as Sidi Zitoun and Soap sold their least valuable pieces—machine-made nylon rugs 3 feet by 6 feet—to tourists for 55 US dollars apiece. Later, when I expressed astonishment at the exorbitant price, the pair laughed saying, "we sell the same crap to Japanese tourists for 300 US dollars!"

On another occasion, two young Canadian women were spotted, wandering around in the medina. One of the guides made a successful snag and gained their confidence; he eventually brought them to Al Malik's shop. They looked over the *kilim* and *zarbia* on

---

[38]There are certain cafés where men publicly smoke hashish or leaf marijuana, *kif*, and there is no particular opprobrium associated with this activity. This is an activity reserved for those too old to work, a pleasure of *la retraite*.

display, and Sidi Zitoun could tell that one of the women really liked one of his least valuable pieces. Setting the table, as it were, he proceeded to extol the virtues of a more expensive one instead. The Canadian eventually bought it at a price that was, unbeknownst to her, scandalously low, affording very little profit for all concerned. Their guide was upset, but Sidi Zitoun told him to relax. Later that afternoon, Sidi Zitoun dispatched one of the younger assistants to find the Canadian women and their guide, and bring them back once more to the killing floor. Amazingly (to me), this was easily accomplished and when they arrived, Sidi Zitoun greeted them with contrition, saying that he had given them a bad deal on the carpet they had bought from him. In an effort to correct this error, he would now offer them a better price for the one they had really preferred all along. The women agreed, and exchanged the more valuable carpet they had bought cheaply for the cheaper less valuable one, having payed Sidi Zitoun four times its value, thereby increasing everyone's *jabba* ("cut" or "take" from a transaction).

While such impressive profits are not as common as more modest takes, one wonders why people pay so much. I suspect it is partly because they are lied to: "these carpets are made of pure silk. . ." But more importantly, it is because they like what they see in the context of the bazaar. The same rug elsewhere would surely be much less attractive without the medina's exoticism and the thrill of interacting with swarthy vendors speaking a "guttural" tongue. The transaction would simply lack the seductive "magic" the tourist seeks.

Moroccans I met live in what has often been called a "shame culture" (Misheva 2000). Public humiliation is to be avoided if at all possible. One's reputation is all one can really claim. Exploitation like that practiced by the guides produces real shame. The guides I know were generally seen as "bad elements" by the upstanding solid citizens and pious proletariat alike. The guides know they are bad. Many revel in their badness. Some, like my friend Sidi Zitoun, walk a tightrope between outward conformity and semi-private debauchery. He takes his meals with his parents when it is convenient for him to do so while hiding his penchant for smoking hashish, drinking alcohol, dating Euro-American women, and indulging in pre-marital heterosexual sex—all of which are frowned upon more or less severely by Fez's faithful. Most guides and merchants catering to the tourist trade try carefully to maintain similar distinctions with more or less success. Publicly they conform to cultural expectations just enough so that they cannot be publicly criticized, yet they indulge themselves when out of the culture's "public eye." It is, however, functionally impossible to be invisible. Herein lies a contradiction, a conflict between conformity and desire.

One whom I will call Mustapha was among those most pleased by teaching me obscene words. He is an outwardly conformist Muslim. He indulges in all the illicit pleasures the tourists come to Morocco to enjoy; he smokes hashish, cigarettes, and kif, gets drunk, and lusts after carefree romance. For him as well as others, the border separating acceptable and unacceptable "lifestyle choices"—or even indulging in the concept of a "lifestyle choice"—is the degree to which one feels compelled to maintain a façade of piety. Though here too there are exceptions.

One afternoon I was on the rooftop of Al Malik's shop in the company of a certain merchant engaged in the tourist trade. The call to prayer was reverberating throughout the city's tracery of corridors and plazas but this man ignored it and his bellowing to friends below on the street actually drowned out the local mosque's *muezzin*. He was shouting for someone to bring him more hashish, of all things!

So on one level these are delinquents who have grown up and now occupy a tolerated place in the community mainly because they commit "victimless" petty fraud and earn a reasonable income by doing so; money that they freely spend throughout the community. At the same time, they are stigmatized and regarded with suspicion by tourist and Moroccan alike.

CHAPTER 9

Unmet Expectations

Kiss any arm you cannot break and pray to God to break it.

—MAALOUF (1984:41)

Since independence in 1954, and as recently as 1994, Morocco has experienced serious protests against symbols representing the government. Young people have been very much at the center of these disturbances. This unrest is not unique to Morocco. It is shared by the other countries of the Maghrib, but until Algeria annulled the results of the 1992 elections and militarily installed a secular regime, the Moroccan demonstrations against the government in Rabat were the most acute in North Africa. Although the violence required to suppress these recurrent protests has been far greater in Algeria, the Moroccan case has not been without mass killings of youths, angry at their leaders for misleading them. For example, in June of 1981 anxiety arising from political and economic austerity measures, undertaken at the behest of foreign creditors, resulted in mass protests in Casablanca. The riots were directed against banks, car dealers, and other businesses identified with elite privilege. Young men from the city's sprawling shantytowns filled the streets and fought with police and military support units for several days. Shots were fired directly into crowds of protesters, killing as many as 200, although some estimates put the death toll much higher.

In January of 1984, violence erupted again over similar grievances. The government announced that basic commodity prices would rise.

Clearly the poor would bear the brunt of the burden. Relatively limited disturbances began in Marrakech, initiated by high school students who were afraid that their registration fees would be increased. They were soon joined by students at the university, by adults, and by unemployed youth from poorer neighborhoods. Protests continued for several weeks into the New Year, and then spread to Agadir, Safi, and other towns in the south, as well as to Rabat and Meknès. According to Tessler (1993) the worst violence occurred in Nador and other cities of the Mediterranean littoral where offices of the national airline, Royal Air Maroc, were attacked along with other symbols of elite indulgence like banks and rental car agencies. Tessler cites Spanish press reports which estimated the number of deaths resulting from the January riots to be as many as 200.

More recently, in December of 1990 riots erupted in Fez over government announcements that food subsidies were to be drastically cut in response to pressure from the IMF and World Bank (*The Economist* 12/22/1990). Police and military were used to subdue the protesters who had attacked buses, banks, businesses associated with consumer goods of foreign manufacture, and significantly, a luxury hotel which was burned to the ground. Official accounts of the level of violence brought to bear are discredited by eyewitness accounts. One informant tried to convey a sense of the event by telling me, "it was a crazy time, everybody was crazy, laughing, burning, looting. The bank was wide open. X and Y walked right in and took the carpets from inside, just walked out with them! Of course, later they were caught and put in jail."

Though Morocco's youth are not the only members of society who are willing to protest against such serious social problems as poverty, injustice, and corruption, they are, or are presumed to be, the most dangerous and volatile, for they have no stake in the status quo, nor have they hopes for their futures. Yet, while the sources of this hopelessness and cynicism are not hard to find, civil disobedience has never resulted in revolution in Morocco. Indeed, according to Entelis, "[t]he overwhelming majority of Moroccans are indifferent to but not ignorant of politics... for most, 'politics' is either irrelevant or insignificant" (1989:45).

In the years immediately following independence (in 1956), the young men and women of Morocco were the source of Moroccan pride, members of a new political generation, who would transform their country into a modern nation. In other words, by virtue of their political, demographic, and intellectual weight they would contribute to the future of a new nation. This hope was not altogether unfounded, given the proportion of those under thirty years of age in the population (see Table 1).

With high rates of growth, the age distribution of the population was strongly skewed in favor of the young. By the early 1970's this rapidly expanding population would come to be recognized as less of a boon than a serious burden. They comprised an obstacle to development as economic gains were undercut by the needs of a booming population whose young clamored for the jobs that Morocco's state-led growth strategy could not provide. Initially, however, following liberation from the French Protectorate, this was not an issue of concern.

The decade following independence was a time of high hopes all across the countries of Northwest Africa (*al maghrib*): Morocco, Algeria, and Tunisia. The generation of young women and men coming of age at this time was better educated, more numerous, and stood to gain greater control of its governing institutions than ever before. As Mattson opined in 1971, "the young Arabs approaching adulthood... will increasingly determine the outcome of competing

TABLE 1. Morocco's population distribution by age.

Year	Total Pop.	% Under 15	% Under 20	% Under 25	% Under 30
1960	11,626,232	44	50	58	67
1971	15,153,608	46	56	63	69
1989	24,570,000	42	51	61	68
		% Under 14	% age 15–64		
2002*	31,167,783	33.8	61.5		

(United Nations Demographic Yearbook, 1990). Data for each successive age group is expressed as a cumulative percentage.
*Source: CIA World Fact Book, 2002.

trends... the new generation will be seeking social status and a meaningful identity as Arabs. Perhaps they will offer an original kind of neo-nationalism, or perhaps neo-Arabism, or, conceivably, why not, of neo-traditionalism" (Mattson, 1971:13). Brik Oussaid (1983:Introduction) put it more bluntly in the preface to his autobiography, "The fact that my book is openly sold in my country in itself represents hope for the future. I need to believe that tomorrow a more merciful and more generous sun will rise over the *Toubkal* [the highest peak in the High Atlas mountains] and the world." And yet there were structural limits to what these young people would be able to achieve in terms of social mobility, limits most people preferred to ignore.

One such limit was employment: the jobs needed to sustain such optimism were not being created. The government did not manage to produce jobs on a scale necessary to accommodate the growing population's needs or aspirations. A growth rate of 3% per annum was ruinous (Ashford 1961). In 1962 urban unemployment was estimated at 14–15% (Tessler 1993:81). Additionally, the seasonal nature of rural employment suggested that large numbers of Moroccans were underemployed.[39] More troubling than rural underemployment was the fact that the burden of unemployment fell most heavily on the shoulders of the young for whom expectations were so high.

Another limit was education. While primary schools were expanding rapidly to meet basic educational needs, access to secondary and tertiary level education was not being made correspondingly available. "June 1962 was nearing. The school year had been a difficult one for my parents, who were no longer able to pay the exorbitant fees. So for the past three years I had no longer been entitled to meals in the canteen, notebooks, or other necessities" (Oussaid 1983:70). Oussaid survived because he was exceptionally intelligent, eventually gaining post-graduate training. But many, many others less fortunate were forced to drop out after only their sixth year. As of 1989, only 36% of children between the

---

[39] I take this to be less serious than the political scientists seem to, for there are concrete benefits to be realized by not devoting oneself to the market body and soul. Moreover, by not working in officially recognized capacities, one is less constrained by the corruption endemic to such occupations.

TABLE 2. Morocco's school enrollment ratios.

Level/Age	1965	1967	1971	1974	1977	1980	1983	1989
Primary 7–11 yrs.	60	55	53	56	69	78	86	68
Secondary 12–18 yrs.	10	12	13	15	19	25	29	36
University	-	-	1.5	-	4.2	6	6.7	11

(United Nations 1990). Enrollment ratio is obtained by dividing the number of students enrolled by the total school-age population.

ages of twelve and eighteen were attending school (see Table 2). And as recently as 1995, only 43.7% of those over age 15 could read and write (CIA 2002).

This is especially troubling because primary schooling alone is insufficient to prepare students to become responsible citizens, not to mention instilling the values inherent in abstractions like "competitiveness" in an increasingly information-driven industrial revolution. Ironically, the bare minimum of education is quite sufficient to afford young people the ability to comprehend just how shut out they really are from the benefits of the global economy. This was clear to Ashford in 1973, who noted that on the whole, schools made no attempts to prepare students for the realities of underemployment (he called it "increased lower-level education"), and that these problems were intensifying (Ashford 1967:257).

Unmet expectations led many young Moroccans to express concern regarding the results of so-called development and their increasingly uncertain prospects. Political apathy and an overwhelming sense of helplessness in the face of corruption and elite control became increasingly common. According to Pascon and Bentahar's 1969 study of rural Moroccan youth, "a formidable desire for change has been overtaken by a profound dissatisfaction, a deep disappointment." Statements similar to one respondent's sentiment can still be heard today among the guides of Fez as well as the students at Fez's Mohammed V

University: "We put children in school for five years and then reject them as if they had never gone" (Pascon and Bentahar, 1972:166–169).

Things have not improved since that statement was uttered and recorded for posterity. In fact, the situation has worsened dramatically. The riots of 1981 and 1984 are evidence that many thousands of young Moroccans have lost their faith in secular institutions, their "solutions," and the claims made for them at Independence as the sources of prosperity and plenty. Rioting alone, however, tells only part of the story.

The difficulties of everyday life, fuel for smoldering resentment expressed through the vehicle of violence directed against an unjust state, can be understood more clearly still by even a cursory glance at the results of a household survey conducted in December 1984 by *Le Matin du Sahara* ("Sahara Morning," a bland, francophone, monarchist newspaper published in Casablanca). Their figures show urban unemployment at 18.4%; 45% of those with jobs were unskilled or semi-skilled laborers.[40] What is more troublesome still was their finding that 79.3% of the active (working) urban population was either functionally illiterate, or had not gone beyond a primary school education. One can assume that these figures have changed only for the worse, with greater and greater numbers of rural Moroccans flocking to the cities of Casablanca, Marrakech, Fez, and Nador in search of opportunities that do not exist. Fifty percent of Morocco's labor force is employed in the agricultural sector (CIA 2003). When the rains fail or are insufficient, people leave the countryside to search for work in the cities.

In short, the government has not been able to create new employment, nor has it been capable of expanding educational opportunities beyond primary school, opportunities that can keep pace with the needs of a rapidly expanding population. Among the foreseeable results are unemployment figures routinely as high as 25% (Parker 1984:17)—or higher, depending upon whom

---

[40]Although as Braverman (1975) has argued, these categories are vague, and can often obscure distinct skill sets. This is quite certainly the case with Fez's unofficial guides to the old city.

one asks.⁴¹ Indeed, estimates of those without regular work, among urban men under 30 years of age without schooling beyond the primary level, range up to 40%. Based on numerous conversations I had with students at Fez's Mohammed V University, regular employment is as hard to find as the Shi'ite's Hidden *Imam*. They have a joke about unemployment:

> Ahmed, who is out of work, is sitting at a café, nursing his demitasse of espresso, when he notices a man step out of his car parked in front of the café. A *one*-dirham *coin (at current rates of exchange, worth roughly ten cents, but in terms of purchasing power, approximately equivalent to one dollar) falls from the man's pocket and rolls under the car. Ahmed decides to wait until the man returns and drives off so that he can recover the money himself. Hours later, when the man finally pulls out and drives away, everyone in the café dives for the coin...*

While some have used the metaphor of a time bomb to describe the conjunction of rapid population growth and slow economic growth (Joffé 1992:141), I think the metaphor is too dramatic. To judge from the last twenty years of post-Independence history's cycles of riots and repression, it would be more accurate to conclude that rebellion in the form of desperate attempts to assert pent-up desires will sporadically flare up, only to be crushed in the most brutal ways available, thereby feeding the cycle anew. The metaphor I find most apt is that of a brush-fire, burning just out of control: each time it is put out, new flames appear elsewhere, yet the overall conflagration is sufficiently removed from threatening the homes of the well-to-do that it can be ignored and left to the "experts'" to "manage."

In Morocco, limited social mobility and associated frustrations have led not only to apathy and non-specific anger directed at symbols of privilege and power, but to increased religious expression as well, and also to consequent alienation from politics-as-usual, by both monarchist and democratic elements. According to Tessler (1982:78–79), the decade from the mid-1960's to the mid-1970's was one of extreme student protest. In 1965, high school and university students, joined by unemployed young men, rioted in the streets of Casablanca. Violence escalated

---

⁴¹The most recent official estimates (1999) put the current unemployment rate at 23% (CIA 2002).

CHAPTER 9: **Unmet Expectations**

to the point that "order" was restored only after the army was deployed and student leaders were arrested. In 1971 and early 1972 student strikes prompted another round of arrests and the closure of most branches of University Mohammed V. Toward the latter part of the 1970's, public demonstrations became less common and leaders less outspoken. The government relaxed political controls somewhat and allowed competitive multi-party elections in 1976 and 1977. This must not be understood as "calm," however, for a survey carried out in 1978–1979 reported that most university students judged the government to be "unresponsive" to the nation's needs. Most also regarded the country's political institutions with contempt. Favoritism and patronage effectively undermined the concessions made to quasi-pluralistic legislative elections, and democratic means were essentially unable to achieve real political goals (Nedelcovych and Palmer 1982).

The lack of participation and the fatalistic attitudes held toward democracy among Morocco's youth is deeply worrisome. According to Suleiman, who conducted surveys of students in Rabat, Casablanca, and Marrakesh (1987:115), young people in Morocco tend to be well informed and quite interested in politics, yet are unlikely to actually participate by voting or other means of public political discourse. Suleiman's findings suggest that among those who are well educated, unwillingness to participate in "legitimate" political institutions is a result of a clear recognition that the government is not responsive to their needs and demands. Such anti-regime attitudes, together with disinterest in political participation in the existing quasi-democratic state structure, indicate their level of alienation and are also a condemnation of current forms of government in Morocco. The alternatives for the disaffected youth are to identify with antigovernment movements, militant Islamicists, or the Left, and bide their time until opportunities for attacking the present regime present themselves. Or they might simply retreat from political engagement altogether and indulge in sybaritic cynicism (which does not necessarily preclude participation in whatever excitement a demonstration may provide). They thus constitute an anomic interest group and are prime candidates for participation in the major riots that have plagued Morocco in the recent past, and may well continue to do so for the foreseeable future.

In Morocco, however, political alienation and the state's formal connection to Islam were intertwined due to the monarchy's fear of communism. In order to neutralize the student movements of the late 1960's and early 1970's, and to crush the communist parties which were formed after Independence, Morocco's government undertook what Tozy (1993) has called "very dangerous manipulations of religion." Specifically, the Moroccan Islamic Youth (*al-Shabiba al-Islamiya*) organization was encouraged and financially supported by the government in 1973, as a counterbalance to increasingly violent urban youth and to turn their attention from what was considered to be potentially dangerous communist ideology. In retrospect, this strategy has generated even greater problems.

> *The contemporary world has left the industrial era behind and entered a new era in which both social relationships and international affairs are being transformed {by} the emergence of these {fundamentalist} religious movements. They are true children of our time: unwanted children, perhaps, bastards of computerization and unemployment or of the population explosion and increasing literacy…*
>
> —KEPEL (1994:11)

Recently and perhaps more ominously for tourists and ordinary Moroccans, protests have shifted from being directed against symbols of elite privilege to being against persons; specifically, secular or non-practicing Muslims. Protests started out based on frustrated secular aspirations (or a desire for western style development and modernity), but now have begun to move away from demands for modernity and toward a politically charged version of Islam. During the time I spent in Fez, there were several riots at the Fez campus of Mohammed V University. The riots erupted between those who were identified colloquially as the "*Ikhwan*" or Brothers, and the non-practicing, or secular, Muslim students. Though none were killed, there were at least seven casualties. These resulted from the fights among students themselves. Police units merely watched as the students fought each other. These events went officially unreported. I learned of them only because some of my friends and informants attended classes there.

According to Zerrouky (2003) in 2002 members of *Assirat el Moustaqim* under the direction of Miloudi Zakaria, and of *Salafia*

Jihadia led by Abdelouhab Fakiri of Fez, carried out at least three assassinations of people in Casablanca they described as "leftist atheists." On February 23, 2002 police discovered the corpse of a man beaten to death after having been named in a *fatwa* by Zakaria. Four months later Zakaria's followers were blamed for a public execution. In September of 2002 the headless torso of a 36-year-old woman was discovered in a trash bag. Moroccan police estimate that members of these organizations number in the thousands. Murders like these have become commonplace occurrences in Algeria, but Morocco has been thought to be somehow immune to the violence that has overwhelmed its neighbor to the East. Clearly, things have changed.[42]

Targeting tourism is one aspect of this change. In 1997, terrorists attacked tour buses at the Temple of Queen Hatshepsut near Egypt's Valley of the Kings at Luxor, killing 58 people and seriously impacting tourism to that country. In Tunisia the tourist destination of Djerba (famous for being the Land of the Lotus Eaters mentioned in Homer's *Odyssey*) was attacked in April 2002. The more recent bombings in Casablanca are being regarded with grave countenances within Morocco's tourism industry. Among the more revealing reports after the May 16, 2003 bombings in Casablanca, Qatar's *The Peninsula* (5/19/2003) reported that:

> *"Since September 11 (2001) and the events of Iraq we lost about 10 per cent of our business," said regional tourism council president Kamel Bensouda. American tourist arrivals dropped by some 26 percent from January through*

---

[42]L'islamisation à marche forcée du Maroc, sous l'oeil complaisant des autorités, a préparé le terrain à l'émergence de ces groupes radicaux. Car, pour de nombreux intellectuels et partis de gauche marocains, obnubilés par la crise du Sahara occidental et par la prétendue menace de l'Algérie, l'islamisme n'était pas pris au sérieux. Au nom d'une certaine "exception marocaine", il était de bon ton de considérer l'islamisme marocain comme étant différent de ses homologues algérien et plus généralement arabes, et même de le considérer comme parfaitement soluble dans la société marocaine, en marche vers la démocratie et le progrès. Certes, des quotidiens et des hebdomadaires comme "Le Journal," "Demain," "Maroc Hebdo" ne cessaient d'attirer l'attention. Sans être écoutés. La menace était tue, enfouie, voire censée émaner de l'extérieur. Après les services algériens, accusés en 1994 d'avoir manipulé les auteurs des attentats de Marrakech, c'est Al Qaida qui est aujourd'hui mise en avant *(Zerrouky 2003).*

October 2002 from the same period in 2001, according to official figures, a worrying development in a sector seen as a key to Morocco's development over the next decade. "It's a disaster for tourism for the country in general and for Casablanca in particular," said Khalid Boukhari, marketing director at the Farah Hotel, one of the targets of the attacks Friday in the heart of Morocco's economic capital. Jalila Ait Ba, who heads a tourist agency in Casablanca, said all of Morocco's main tourist destinations—Fez, Marrakesh, Agadir as well Casablanca—would be affected. "Tourists don't distinguish between the north and south of a country once it is considered dangerous. ... And in our case, our Algerian and Tunisian neighbours are already considered countries at risk," she said.

Nevertheless, the Moroccan government is trying to be reassuring. For example, on his 2003 trip to Paris, France, Moroccan Premier Driss Jettou was quoted by *Maghreb Arabe Presse* as saying that Morocco faces no threat of "Islamic extremism." "No [such] danger is looming in Morocco," said Jettou after a meeting with French assembly member Jean-Pierre Raffarin. Two days later, on June 18th, Moody's Investor Services upgraded Morocco's foreign currency country ceiling and local currency government bond rating from "negative" to "stable" (*Middle East North Africa Financial Network* 6/19/03).

CHAPTER 9: **Unmet Expectations**

Chapter 10

The Nature of Authenticity

Because Fez is such a confusing compound of disarming simplicity and unfathomable complexity, it has called forth a complete library of interpretive opinion of the most divergent views. Travelers either love Fez or they fear it. One tourist sees a prince of the blood bestride a fat brown mule, cantering in reckless glory down a narrow street, with a black slave in magenta pantaloons running alongside, one hand on a silver stirrup, one hand waving away the lesser mortals... and this for him, is Fez—the city of Arabian Nights pageantry. He is the tourist who goes rapturously sniffing through the spice bazaars, who follows tattered little baker-boys as they carry on their heads six-foot planks piled high with bread to be baked in the public ovens, who prowls eternally in the dim gabled alleys of Fez like a lover, fearless and insatiate. Another tourist, remembering doubtless all the bloody history he had read of Fez, sees naught but frenzy, fanaticism and imminent revolt seething just under the surface. The lusty bargaining of Moroccan merchants makes him think the war has already started. The unrelenting surge of pilgrims toward mosques and shrines frightens him, and the muted roar coming up from the souks makes him think twice and hire a guide before attempting a timorous trip downhill. He is the tourist who is too afraid of Fez to revel in it, who looks upon its impenetrable face and finds the sharp live features dim and dying in the twilight of Islam. In reality, Fez was never farther from its twilight than it is today. It has merely shut its gates on the passing centuries and drawn its sustenance from some rich substratum of medieval understanding. The shining electric

> *wires strung above the Arab rooftops are the only reminders that we live in the twentieth century. Remove these few threads of testimony, and one could be living in a fifteenth-century city of colorful pageantry, of fervid artistic achievement and of dynamic spiritual and intellectual activity.*
>
> —Hulme (1930:24)

> *Since we all participate on teams we must all carry within ourselves something of the sweet guilt of conspirators. And since each team is engaged in maintaining the stability of some definitions of the situation, concealing or playing down certain facts in order to do this, we can expect the performer to live out his conspiratorial career in some furtiveness.*
>
> —Goffman (1959:105)

The social context of activity or inquiry determines knowledge, or understanding of reality, and not the world as it is (Kant's *Dinge-an-sich*). Therefore knowledge is understood to be always relative to its social setting, and as the product of on-going and active *bricolage* rather than as the discovery of reality always-already there. As Karl Marx wrote in his preface to *A Contribution to the Critique of Political Economy*:

> *In the social production of their life, men enter into definite relations that are indispensable and independent of their will, relations of production which correspond to a definite stage of development of their material productive forces. The sum total of these relations of production constitutes the economic structure of society, the real foundation, on which rises a legal and political superstructure and to which correspond definite forms of social consciousness. The mode of production of material life contains the social, political and intellectual life process in general.* It is not the consciousness of men that determine their being, but, on the contrary, their social being that determines their consciousness. *At a certain stage of their development, the material productive forces of society come in conflict with the existing relations of production, or—what is but a legal expression for the same thing—with the property relations within which they have been at work hitherto. From forms of development of the productive forces these relations turn into their fetters. Then begins an epoch of social revolution. With the change of the economic foundation the entire immense superstructure is more or less rapidly transformed. In considering such transformations a distinction should always be made between the material transformation of the economic conditions of*

> *production, which can be determined with the precision of natural science, and the legal, political, religious, aesthetic or philosophic—in short, ideological forms—in which men become conscious of this conflict and fight it out (1977:4–5 emphasis added).*

This is certainly the case when it comes to the ways that guides in Fez earn their livelihood, and also the ways in which they interacted with me.

I was intimidated in some way or other on a daily basis by the guides individually, or as a group, during my stay in Fez, Morocco. I was judged a nuisance, patron, failure, and friend by any given one of my informants depending upon the nature of our relations (ongoing or historical) up to the moment of the interaction of any given day. This is not to say that at all times all informants threatened me, making me uncomfortable. No, it is rather that expectations of me were frequently impossible to meet. This produced differing reactions among the Moroccans I came to know closely and peripherally. In fact, their expectations often dictated the proximity of my relations with them, such as how much time I would spend with them and for what reasons and purposes.

According to the amorphous body of theory collectively referred to as Symbolic Interactionism, meaning arises through social interaction, and the social world itself is a social product (Blumer 1969). Useful analogies include a conversation, a drama, or more problematically, a text. Craib (1984) writes, "the social world shows the same qualities of flow, development, creativity and change as we would experience in a conversation… [indeed] the world is made up of conversations, internal and external." Goffman (1959) describes an enacted reality constructed by individuals out of an infinite set of possibilities. Geertz (1983) describes a "refiguration of social thought" around the interpretation of social life conceived as, among other things, a text.[43]

---

[43] I am not particularly inclined to accept this analogy, however. A joke illustrates this best: a post-modern theorist delivers a lecture entitled "War as Text." Afterwards a member of the audience asks if the theorist would be willing to deliver the same lecture to the Veterans of Foreign Texts...

Despite criticisms of "deliberately constructed vagueness" (Rock and Downes 1985), I take from Symbolic Interactionism an emphasis upon what Craib (1984:73) distills into three basic postulates. First, people act towards things based upon what these things mean to them. Second, these meanings are the direct result of social interaction with other people in society. And third, these meanings are acted upon and used in a process of interpretation every person engages in as they encounter the signs and symbols of daily life. These guiding concepts essentially correspond to the three sections of Mead's posthumously published lectures, *Mind, Self and Society* (1934).

Within anthropology, geography, and sociology Symbolic Interactionist perspectives have produced considerable insight, generating essentially three directions of inquiry in ever-widening scope. First, the ethnographic tradition of the Chicago School continues to thrive, providing convincing accounts of how social construction operates in specific settings (Denzin 1992, Ferrell and Hamm 1998, Jackson 1985, McMurray 2001). Second, a rigorous examination of the social construction of place has emerged. An example is Ley's argument that "[P]lace is a negotiated reality, a social construction by a purposeful set of actors. But the relationship is mutual, for places in turn develop and reinforce the identity of the social group that claims them" (1981). Third, encompassing the two previous directions of inquiry, efforts have also been aimed at offering a set of umbrella concepts concerning how society is ordered. As Duncan observes,

> *Interactionism... posits no separation between the individual and society; individual selves are socially constructed. The self is largely a product of the opinions and actions of others as these are expressed in interaction with the developing self... With interactionism there is no need for a transcendental object such as an abstract notion of culture {or} society to mediate between the individual and society (1978:269).*

Composing a "taken-for-granted" world, these social constructions are at least in part "dependent on one's relations to a place and the persons associated with that place" (Duncan 1978). Of particular relevance to my observations, Duncan points out that by virtue of employing a place-specific perspective when considering "strangers" or "outsiders" one is more likely to notice "the social construction of unreality" (Duncan 1978). This is supported by Berger and Luckmann's eponymous *The Social Construction of Reality* (1967). Specifically, in recognizing the importance of routine and repetitive social contacts for maintaining the continuity of social life, they write "[t]he reality of everyday life maintains itself by being embodied in routines, which is the essence of institutionalization. Beyond this, however, the reality of everyday life is ongoingly reaffirmed in the individual's interaction with others" (1967:169).

Once I had come to understand the fact that context—including the ancient city itself—could be manipulated to serve the ends of my informants, I realized the importance of "authenticity." Popular accounts, especially travel literature, frequently assert the goal or achievement of discovering the "real"—the authentic—Morocco. For example:

> *Tidy Europe, 1998, had left me restless. So I fled south to Morocco, land of voluptuous anarchy... {W}eaving in and out of the crowd are those hucksters against whom the tourist manuals warned me... 'Let me show you the real Morocco,' he says... I accept Rachid's invitation to the medina of Fez, a place where at the time foreigners rarely found accommodation... To reach Rachid's home, deep within a honeycomb of squalid dwellings, we navigate—he nimbly, I haltingly—endless unlighted lanes, stairs, ladders, and planks. No stranger could unearth this rickety route. Without question, I'm in the real Morocco.*
>
> —KRAUS (2001)

Or,

> *High in Morocco's mountains, my three friends and I had found what we were looking for: still, open spaces, and a palette of muted pastels that seemed to flush away the polluted grays of our urban lives.*
>
> —DOLAND (2001)

And,

> *I'd come to Fez to get lost in the ultimate urban anachronism: a city whose convoluted corridors were barely wide enough for donkeys and bakers to pass, a political entity organized by buildings of prayer (but where trade and commerce are all), a place where in the words of its own promoters, 'there is*

no distinguishable borderline between pleasures that are of the mind and pleasures that are of the senses'.

—BROWNING (1996)

In short, I discovered that there is no such thing as authenticity.[44] There is not a "real Morocco" as is so regularly mentioned in popular accounts of travels or acquisitions among tourists and travelers, nor is there a "real America" for that matter.

I do not intend to pose a philosophical question and argue along with the Sophists that all is illusion, but rather it seems to me that all is relative or contextual. Certainly my pocket watch is real in the sense that it keeps time when wound properly, and is a genuine product of the now-defunct Waltham Watch Company. But its authenticity—its genuineness, its existence as it seems to be—is utterly relative when discussion of its value is taken up. And herein lies the problem: just as A. J. P. Taylor once argued that the battles of El Alamein or Stalingrad only became authentic when they appeared on the cinema screen, so the value of my pocket watch is only authenticated when I extol its virtues in relation to other pocket watches (this is especially so if there happens to be someone else of like mind who appreciates antique mechanical pocket watches, in which case we share what some would surely refer to as "intersubjectivity"). The real Morocco—or America, or anywhere—is then to be found everywhere within the locale being described, in the seamy slums of Casablanca's *bidonvilles*, just as in those of Fez. Yet for travelers and tourists alike, the exotic is the "reality" they have come for—an "authentic" experience is what they have saved up for, and intend to spend their treasure on, to own as a memory, a souvenir.

---

[44] "The tourist and the terrorist—those twin ghosts of the airports of abstraction—suffer an identical hunger for the *authentic*. But the authentic recedes as they in their inauthenticity approach it... To their secret misery, all they can do is destroy. The tourist destroys *meaning* and the terrorist destroys the tourist" (Bey 1999).

CHAPTER 11

Seeking Authenticity

You're much more likely to find the real Fès by letting your senses lead you slowly through the crowded bazaars, pausing whenever the mood takes you to watch something of interest, rummage through the articles for sale, or simply sit down with a glass of tea and take it all in.

—Morocco (1998:279)

For many, the authentic souvenir object from Fez is a carpet such as those sold by Al Malik. He and his associates live in what for those who have never seen Fez, must seem like a scene from Sinbad's adventures. In order to reach Al Malik's shop you have to negotiate a narrow alley that descends at a 15% grade and, as you pass under an archway, you turn right onto a narrower alley.

Here you are assaulted not only by the smells of rotten sewage, but also by the sullen stares of shopkeepers who sit idly in their woolen hooded gowns and yellow leather slippers, occasionally murmuring to a neighbor a few yards off in his shop. Children in the midst of raucous play suddenly stop and stare. A stranger, a *nisrani* (Christian, generic term for foreigner) no less, is not a welcome presence—except to Al Malik who gets to his feet and warmly ushers the potential customer up the narrow, twisting, uneven staircase into his carpet bazaar. A single electric bulb casts a pallid light over the walls of rough plaster and the ceiling of rough-hewn timbers, of which one catches a glimpse between the vibrantly colored carpets that hang from nails and cover every square inch of wall space. Low benches run the length of the room against three of the four walls. An adjoining, smaller room is similarly decorated. And near the stairway, at the entrance end of the room sits a rickety loom, at which Driss pushes the pedals with his bare feet alternating the warp and woof of his creation as the shuttle passes from side to side.

This is the killing floor for Al Malik and his crew of guides. Here is where the deal is consummated or, if not, chalked up to what they all refer to as "*kul habibi*" which means literally to eat one's love. In the less idiomatic form, it means simply that any investment in the lost deal is merely the cost of doing business. It is the multiple meanings of this selling space within the larger context of Fez itself that I am interested in discovering. They are not absolutes; but rather reflect the contexts in which they are conveyed. For their clients, tourist guides define meanings of the settings and interactions they experience. They do so, in particular ways, to suit their own purposes. For the guides, the tourist clients are merely the means to an end. Sales equal profits that they can use to purchase status items they covet, repay debts they have accrued, buy drugs they enjoy, and in all cases give money to their parents. Or so goes the line offered to the likes of me. From experience I have little reason to doubt the claim.

For those who see Fez's alleys, Al Malik's shop, and in fact all of Morocco, as more generally exotic, these scenes are ironically, unreal. That is, they experience an authentic feeling of being in an utterly strange place, and their guide convinces them of its authenticity by referring to the location's antiquity or by exploiting their client's sense of confusion amid the maze of alleys ("could you find your way out of here without me to guide you?" With the implication that most probably they could not, especially if they do not speak French or Arabic). Yet the city is obviously not the least bit strange to those who live there. To them the tourist who marvels at the sights is as silly as the country bumpkin who cranes his neck to see the tops of skyscrapers. Or worse, as one informant told me, many tourists are regarded as a disappointment when compared with the Euro-Americans they have seen in movies and on television. They are often scruffy and dirty. "They do things here [in Fez] they don't do at home." Switching to

French, she added, *"C'est lui qui méprise les autres. Ils manquent de respect."*

The carpets sold as antiques, or of "tribal" origin, are mostly produced expressly for the tourist market, and as such are not "authentic." They are real (just like my pocket watch), but they are not antiques, they have little value—though many vendors go to great lengths to hide that fact.[45] Without exception, all the carpets sold by vendors like Al Malik come from squalid factories, often woven by young girls.

Tourists and tour guides are an extremely heterogeneous and diverse group of independent and interdependent agents. It is not an oversimplification to claim that:

> *Tourist fantasy permits the self to assume diverse social roles in exotic settings; tourism invents and demands empathy to play out short-term fantasy roles. Tourism tends to make cultures into museums, as cultural phenomena which can be viewed as quaint, peculiar and local. Tourism paradoxically is a quest for authentic local cultures, but the tourist industry, by creating the illusion of authenticity, in fact reinforces the experience of social and cultural simulation. The very existence of tourism rules out the possibility of authentic cultural experience.*
>
> —TURNER (1994:185)

This is precisely what has happened in Fez. The old city, though still home to a great number of people, can at the same time be regarded as a museum. The products of the men and women who live and work in the old city are both objects for daily use (leather slippers, teapots, brass trays, *djellabas*, etc.) as well as tourist kitsch. The "authentic" experience of Fez *al bali* is hardly different from that of strolling through a shopping mall.

---

[45] An excellent example of the lengths to which merchants will go to forge objects' authenticity comes from Taylor and Barbash's research in West Africa as shown in their film *In and Out of Africa (1992).*

Tourism too is nothing if not kaleidoscopic in its diversity. Ryan (1991) defines tourism as essentially "about the experience of place. The tourism 'product' is not the tourist destination, but it is about experience of that place and what happens there: [which is] a series of internal and external interactions." Or, as Urry (1990:2) put it,

> ...places are chosen to be gazed upon because there is an anticipation... constructed and sustained through a variety of non-tourist practices, such as film, television, literature, magazines, records and videos, which construct and reinforce the gaze... {and} an array of tourist professionals develop who attempt to reproduce ever new objects for the tourist gaze.

Additional characteristics of tourism include transitory relationships which impede mutual understanding between guests and hosts. And, the latter labor while the former enjoy leisure.

According to a Sufi mystic I knew in Fez, "we are in the third stage of the sign." By this he meant that the absence of "basic reality" is hidden by "hyper reality." The latter is made possible by modern communications technology which, in turn, has helped create a new cultural object out of individual consumers who, because they use these communications technologies, also reproduce official ideology in the form of further desire to consume. Desire is insatiable because structurally only very few can achieve the level of material comfort consumer ideology promises. Moreover, the dead world of things cannot provide the emotional solace consumerist ideology promises. The importance of tourism lies in the impact of the experiences sold to whoever can afford them. These experiences are the currency in competitions and conversations with others of similar habitus.[46, 47]

Ironically, for the guides of Fez as well as for their analogs in any of the myriad places that have become tourist destinations, in the

---

[46]Gewertz and Errington describe the competition over claims to authentic experiences they were drawn into with travelers and tourists in Wewak, New Guinea (1989). They conclude that to be of any significance, anthropologists must bend to the task of understanding and describing the political implications of the acquisition of the experiences that tourists and travelers use to trump claims of having "been there."

[47]Habitus can be initially understood as the fundamental building blocks, realized or not, of a person's socialization (Bourdieu 1972).

name of independence and freedom from the restrictive norms of local culture they have become dependent upon outsiders, tourists. In the process of this transformation of dependency from local to global economies, the guides are also exploited. They are vulnerable to the depredations of corrupt police. They work at the whim of fickle tourists. Their freedom is constrained by the psychology of individual tourists as well as the vicissitudes of the global tourism industry.

In an effort to strengthen Berger and Luckmann's insights by taking heed of what C. Wright Mills called "the sociological imagination" (1959), I have attempted to show how everyday intersections of individual biographies with institutional activities in particular places and at particular times expose how society works in Fez, Morocco. I want to avoid the two-dimensional oversimplifications of "the tourist" just as I want to represent the guides as more complex than they may at first seem.

CHAPTER 12

Open Sesame

> *The ethnographer and his subjects are both performers and audience to one another. They have to judge one anothers' motives and other attributes on the basis of short but intensive contact and then decide what definition of themselves and the surrounding situation they want to project; what they will reveal and what they will conceal and how best to do it. Each will attempt to convey to the other the impression that will best serve his interests as he sees them.*
>
> —BERREMAN (1962:11)

I had been hanging around, uncomfortably, with the group of guides who orbited Al Malik's carpet shop for a week or so. Al Malik was already aware of why I wanted to be there, and was all for the idea of allowing me to learn the world of the guide in Fez, "the guiding way," as he put it. But he could not compel the others to feel or act the same way, and many, if not all, were unimpressed by my presence. Some were openly hostile. Hoping that some word or sign from Al Malik would break the ice in my favor, I lamely tried to be friendly toward the boisterous group of young men, smiling and ignoring their increasingly strident insults in French and English. At the time, early in my stay, I did not know enough *Dérija* (Moroccan Arabic dialect) to understand their comments in Arabic. One in particular, *"hissess!"* elicited gales of laughter, especially since my response was to smile and shrug. I later learned that it means, essentially, "queen bottom," the one who is penetrated during male homosexual sex.

As the guides grew rowdier, it became increasingly clear that conciliatory gestures on my part had been a mistake. I realized that, like the guides themselves, I would have to use intimidation or some other direct method to demonstrate that I was a person to be reckoned with, and by so doing achieve my goal—in this case, gaining their confidence and respect so as to learn all I could from them. And it could not wait until the "next time"; it had to be now...

One chap in particular was enjoying himself a great deal at my expense. He was mocking my limited *Dérija* by loudly repeating my words in an exaggerated American accent. I tried to ignore him. He persisted. I tried to be polite. He grew more insistent, standing before me and fairly spitting his insults at me. His parody was bitingly accurate: he copied my body language; he mimicked the typically American tendency to speak more loudly when confronted with someone who does not speak English; he switched to French using the same broad American accent to render his speech hysterically funny to his audience. He had me. Or so it seemed.

I had read a little about the difficulties and importance gaining *entrée*, and knew that success was in no way assured. Too, I was still smarting from the repeated rejections with which my efforts at making contacts with the likes of Abu Bakr had been met. I also knew that my entire project depended upon somehow passing this test. Little I had been taught or read had any practical suggestions for how to deal with the problem of gaining the confidence of those whom an anthropologist wishes to become informants (the glaring exception is Berreman 1962, esp. pp. 12–22). Failure, it would seem, may well happen in science, but not often in ethnography. What to do?

My antagonist, not unlike many young men in Fez, fancied the balletic moves of martial arts. Indeed it was not unusual to see boys acting out by attacking one another with a variety of karate chops and judo throws, copied from the latest Hong Kong thriller at the cinema. Few, if any, of the guides I knew had the means to pursue formal training in such esoterica. My antagonist himself began posturing in just such ways, pretending to throw punches to my face, or aiming a kick at my chest. I ignored the feints, blocked the kicks, and remained as outwardly calm as possible. Something had to be done not only to regain my place as the American guest among them, but also to earn their respect.

In desperation, an idea came to me. I went on the offensive. "*Baraka! Wakha, wakha, yallah!*" (Enough! All right, all right, let's go!) I said firmly and in the clearest *Dérija* I could muster. I grabbed my tormentor in a bear hug, and thus temporarily subdued, I issued a challenge to him. I asked Al Malik to spread a carpet on the floor so no offending dirt could detract from the moment's *gravitas*, and said, "*shoof*" (watch). Silence overcame the room. I lay face-down on the carpet, arms stretched out straight in front of me, and proceeded to do ten push-ups while in the arms-outstretched position. "*Wash kat dir hatha?*" (Can you do that?) I asked. The assembled guides began to hoot and yell, cheering for one of their own, as my erstwhile antagonist was literally called out on the carpet. Affecting indifference, he adjusted himself and assumed the position. After a pregnant pause he tensed with the effort of trying to overcome the force of gravity in this exceedingly awkward pose.

Such a push-up is quite difficult and physically demanding; it requires a strong back and shoulders and triceps. I doubt I could do even one today. But at the time I was fit, and stronger than I looked, thanks to having once been a wrestler and to the fact that I enjoyed strenuous aerobic activities such as running and bicycling in the Berkeley hills.

When it became obvious to all that he could not do a single push-up, never mind matching or beating my efforts, he conceded defeat amid further gales of laughter. But now, the guides were laughing at him, not me. Now each one wanted to know if there was a secret trick to doing push-ups this way (there is not), and most importantly, they wanted to know me and share their thoughts and feelings as equals, members of a select group. I now belonged. Thus began my career among the illegal guides of Fez, Morocco.

I later learned that the man who gave me such a hard time that evening had the revealing sobriquet, "Yeast." "Because," as one guide told me, "he's always puffing himself up." Apparently I had managed to choose the optimal individual ego to "deflate" in order to achieve my end: acceptance by the group.

CHAPTER 13

The Animal and the Scorpion

Depression and gnawing feelings of low mental health were assuaged by the temporary excitement of the ritual process of deviant behavior (planning, acting, fleeing, and talking about it) and the numbing high of drugs and alcohol.

—FLEISHER (1995:118)

Though regularly intimidated, I was never physically afraid in Fez except around two people. One was a person with whom the guides were friendly, and who, I later learned, allegedly killed his father one evening. His nickname is revealing: *Al Hyawan*, the Animal. He had simply stopped showing up, and after a prolonged absence I asked after him. "*Al habs,*" (prison) was the eventual reply. I tried to verify this, but was ignored by the police. The guides insisted it was true: the Animal had killed his father, stabbing him in the eye, because his father refused to accede to the Animal's plan to go to America—Atlantic City, New Jersey to be specific—and pursue a career as a gambler.

It is curious how, when one spends time among people of evil reputation, the hollowness of such reputations becomes clear even as the objective truth of their nastiness may also be apparent. To put it another way, Al Malik and his thieves were never particularly cruel to me, although we fought on occasion. To outsiders perhaps they seemed unsavory ("like grade-B movie bad guys," was how an American friend described them to me after having met Al Malik while visiting me in Fez), but I was consistently impressed by their willingness to treat me with respect—to my face. Behind my back

I suspect that much different feelings were shared regarding my presence among them. For example, it was only by accident that I learned I had been given a nickname that no one ever used to refer to me in person: "Scarface." Despite Fez's rather unsavory reputation, I was known among the guides and *commerçants* of the neighborhood, and hence felt quite at ease. Even the parricidal one who was a leg-breaker for his family's business never threatened me overtly. I feared him because whenever he got an idea (mercifully rare occasions) he was absolutely unreasonable were one to refuse to go along with whatever escapade he had in mind. An infantile enthusiasm for the least practical of adventures characterized his way of being in the world. "Let's go," he would say. "Where to?" I would ask.

"The mountains."

"How will we get there?"

"Al syara," he would condescendingly sneer, using the classical Arabic term for automobile.

"Whose?" I would ask, ignoring the insult.

"Leave it to me."

"OK," was all I could reply without risking further escalation of his impositions upon my peace of mind and physical safety.

Fortunately for me, not only were these sudden inspirations to pursue adventures rare, but when they did occur, a generalized disorganization and lethargy impeded or blunted his charisma and force of will to actually realize his plan. Others felt as I did, and like me were careful not to let it show. The only overt confirmation of this came from Sidi Zitoun one afternoon when he and I were the only ones in the carpet shop. I mentioned the Animal, whereupon Sidi Zitoun rolled his eyes and said only, "*hummuck*" (crazy).

The Scorpion (*al Aqrub*), whom I also feared, was different. Like the Animal, he hailed from a wealthier, older Fassie family. But where the Animal was blunt, the Scorpion was subtle. He pretended to be capable of violence, but when his bluff was called he feigned illness or injury. I never saw him fight. The Scorpion was one of the crew, but he held himself apart. He was haughty and his family's connections were his weapon of choice. He could intimidate others by threatening to use his family's influence to cause unspecified problems for anyone who crossed him. The Scorpion made his words as soft and sweet as he could, saving his venom for the negotiations over his fees and kickbacks. In short, the Scorpion had the greatest amount of self-control and used it to maximize his earning potential.

The Scorpion worked hard to be cool. He memorized the lyrics to American pop tunes and sang them lustily at what seemed to him to be the appropriate moment in a conversation. For example, one afternoon another guide had brought an American couple from the West coast to Al Malik's carpet shop. They seemed interested in a particular rug, but Al Malik would not meet their price. As their irritation with his perceived greedy obstinacy grew, the Scorpion deftly produced a hashish-laced cigarette, lit it, and exhaling the smoke sang in accented English, "You can't always get what you want, but if you try sometimes you get what you need. . ." It broke the tension. The Americans relaxed, smoked, and in due course, Al Malik lowered his price just enough to sell them the carpet they wanted. As he did so, he told their guide (in Arabic) that the commission on this sale would be somewhat reduced to cover the Scorpion's contribution to the deal.

On the rooftop of Al Malik's shop with the Scorpion, Soap, and Muscles one afternoon, *al Aqrub* began teaching me offensive words and phrases. He would think of something like, "your mother fucks dogs" for example, and the others would collapse giggling as I repeated after him. We were seated along the low wall dividing Al Malik's rooftop from the family's next door. I could hear a woman's voice speaking to children. *Al Aqrub* appeared unperturbed by the obvious presence of the woman and her children so nearby and certainly within earshot. Embarrassed but unwilling to let it show lest I be harassed more than usual, I marveled at his willingness to transgress norms of public comportment so blatantly. After ten minutes or so Sidi Zitoun bounded up onto the roof and, instantly comprehending the situation, told the Scorpion to stop such talk immediately. He literally shamed the Scorpion into silence by telling him, "*Hashuma, lay ham walidik*" ("Shame on you, may Allah be of comfort to your parents").

The Scorpion and the Animal represent, for me, two extremes along the spectrum of presentation of self among the guides I came to know, and their associates. Their use of the standard combination of threats, intimidation, and bluffs, as well as praise and flattery, to conduct their business demonstrate the antipodes of a continuum. Both of these men tried to frighten me so as to control me. Each succeeded in his own way.

One day Al Malik invited me to go to the mountains with him, the Scorpion, and another man whom I will call Rachid. Rachid was a curious fellow. He was small even by local standards, and somewhat of an outsider since he was from Casablanca. He was in Fez, under Al Malik's protection, hiding from the police of "Casa" because he was wanted for a knife fight there that had resulted in serious wounds to another man.

We took Scorpion's Renault sedan to a lake in the Ait Youssi region of the Middle Atlas, near Imouzzer-Kandar. After more than an hour's drive, we arrived at a picnic area near a small lake. The mountains were low and covered with sparse firs. Other people had come up to this alpine Shangri-la to escape the oppressive trap of Fez as well. A young couple and an extended family sharing a picnic were at the lakeshore where we stopped for our outing. The parents in the picnicking family were unnerved by our presence, as was the woman of the couple. The parents discouraged their children from even looking at us as we openly swilled red wine and my companions proceeded to get loudly and publicly drunk. The young couple was there to take photographs: he of her from at least 60 to 80 yards away with a massive telephoto lens. She was clearly made nervous by our presence and said so to her photographer-beau. He refused to recognize us as a threat and insisted that she move further and further away from him so he could capture her image surrounded by the low hills and lake with his expensive apparatus.

I felt very embarrassed to be among the three drunkards. But at the same time, I was transfixed by the situation itself (not to mention a little drunk). Here we were, the four of us, publicly contravening the explicit Muslim prohibition on alcohol consumption. With their shouted obscenities, my Moroccan companions were engaging in activity that was blatantly insulting to the others present. They would never have done this in Fez, which is precisely why we had gone all the way to Imouzzer. As they put it, in the "countryside" they were free to bask in their anonymity, whereas in town, everyone knew them.[48] Their witnesses were anonymous and therefore posed negligible risks to my informants' public reputations back in Fez.

We proceeded to drink, finishing several bottles of wine. I ignored my shame of our deviant display. When the wine was gone, and the air began to chill as the sun dropped behind the hills, the group's thoughts turned toward Fez.

Scorpion drove us home in the gathering dusk and eventual deep black of the early spring evening. I sat just behind him. Pleasantly drunk, I did not pay much attention to Scorpion's driving. Al Malik lit a joint and eventually passed it back to Rachid, who eventually passed it to me. There was little left when I was ready to pass it along to Scorpion, so I asked him if he wanted it. He said no, he was just about to light his own. I thought little of it, assuming that Al Malik who was in the passenger seat had rolled it for him. By the time Rachid was ready to pass it to me, Scorpion had another fresh joint going! The roads are very narrow as they wind precipitously along the Middle Atlas and drop down towards the Sais Plain. I began to feel nervous about Scorpion's increasingly reckless driving. He was in the habit of driving without his headlights, a Cairene affectation with which I was familiar, having lived for some time in Cairo where headlights are rarely used; the rationale being that one's headlights blind the oncoming vehicle's operator. But Scorpion was, it seemed to me, tempting fate by purposely driving in the oncoming lane just for kicks. What was worse, he was steering with his knees as he rolled the joints we had all been enjoying together in his car. I became upset when I realized all this.

I insisted that Scorpion drive more carefully. He ignored me. I persisted, and he began teasing me in response, telling me that if we crash it is merely Allah's will. In short, he and the other two, like the majority of my informants, adamantly maintained that there is no such thing as chaos; there is, however, fate. Helpless, I reiterated my demand that Scorpion drive more responsibly. He and the others ignored me and then teased me some more, telling me

---

[48]The countryside, "*al bled,*" is an important symbol of belonging as well as ridicule.

that some things are simply beyond one's control. I could not understand why they did not worry for their own safety. What I later understood of course is that whatever concern they may have had was unseemly, and had to be concealed out of respect for Scorpion. My reaction was not only considered to be hysterical, but insulting. Finally, I threatened to stop the car by taking the keys out of the ignition. I would rather have walked home than be subjected to Scorpion's capriciousness. Scorpion relented, but in doing so managed to maintain control of the situation. He slowed down to a snail's pace. One could have walked faster than he was driving. I was humiliated, defeated. He forced me to agree with him that it was better to allow him to speed up.

Scorpion was a very ambivalent associate of mine. He never consented to an unambiguous "standard" interview. He would often startle me with a flamboyance none of the others would dare exhibit. He delighted in piquing anyone who happened to aggravate him, often for no reason at all. His nickname came from his willingness to attack anyone, without respect for status. A "loose cannon," he reminded me of American *mafiosi* bravado in the face of generalized violence.

CHAPTER 14

The Lynx

"My informants never took personal change seriously."

—FLEISHER (1995:246)

Tall and slim, with green eyes, brown hair, and no moustache, the guide whom I will call the Lynx is a striking figure of a man. He smiles easily, and flashes unusually clean, straight teeth. He pays scrupulous attention to the shine of his shoes, and is fastidious about his appearance. Unlike many of the other guides I knew, the Lynx was always calm and self-contained when savoring his successes or nursing his defeats. I came to know him better than any of the others, and we spent considerable time together.

In total, he and I spent several weeks in the village of his birth. Whenever we left, he told the others that he wanted to visit with his extended family, but the real motive was so that we could talk together without the anxieties of Fez and the omnipresent ears of others inhibiting the free flow of conversation. Each afternoon we were there, we would take our leave of the family and hike several miles to a nearby mountaintop to conduct our interviews.

The Lynx was born in 1966 in a peasant village 25 kilometers from Fez. His father is a laborer. The Lynx spent five years in primary school in his natal village. After the Lynx finished primary school, his father left his mother and moved to a village in the Middle Atlas mountains south of Fez. There he remarried, this time to a much younger woman. The Lynx remained with his mother in the village but, after a year, his mother took his younger sister and left too. Three years later, she returned with a new husband. The Lynx went to his father but his father's new wife did not like him. "I am not her son," he told me. "She wanted me to stop school, to fail." The Lynx was ordered to leave school and tend to his father's livestock. This was a very difficult period for him, because he had truly loved school and remains a very astute and clever person. The Lynx lasted six months in that assignment before losing his father's prized bull. He had gone to a cousin's wedding ceremony instead of minding the animals. At age twelve or thirteen (he is not exactly certain) the Lynx ran away to Fez, and did not see his father again for twelve years. In Fez, the Lynx begged for a place to sleep at the house of his father's brother with whom he had spent summers as a young boy. His uncle agreed, on the condition that the Lynx give up his dream of going to school, and instead work in the brass *souk* of Fez, *al Sefarin*. He obeyed, and managed to earn five and a half *dirhams* per day (roughly sixty cents), keeping only half a *dirham* for himself out of his wages. The rest went to his uncle's household.

At that time he was more interested in the craft, and life itself, than money. He was happy to give his earnings to his uncle. "I had no use for money," he said. After an unspecified period of time—several months—he began working in the leather tanneries selling wallets and ornamental saddlery in a tourist shop. "In 1979 and 1980, not so many guides," he told me as he reminisced about the heyday of guiding in Fez. Few spoke French well. The Lynx had excellent French thanks to his early enthusiasm for school. He began guiding for small change and toys (10 *dirhams*, or kites, soccer balls, etc.).

"I would guide for cigarettes and give them to my uncle. With time, I no longer wanted to do anything but guide. When I was a child everything I was told I accepted [as true]. Not like now. Now you need to give me smoke or wine!" Such are the emoluments the Lynx insists upon, over and above his fees for guiding. He still keeps his few possessions at his uncle's house, and considers it the closest thing he has to a home.

In his new line of work the Lynx met convicts, "strong people" who forced their will on those weaker than themselves, including himself. He worked for them selling carpets, leather goods, or hashish. If he sold five or six kilos of hashish he would earn 300 *dirhams*, or perhaps be given a kilo of hashish for himself to smoke and/or sell. He worked three years for one group, then another five years for others. He regularly sold ten to fifteen carpets each week. "It was like travelling for me," he explained. By guiding tourists he was able to feel free from the constraints of poverty and expected norms of behavior.

According to the Lynx, having no mother gave him a special concern for, and sensitivity to, the relationship between one's honor and social mistakes. He was exceedingly careful to learn from mistakes, his own and those of others, and assiduously avoided errors. "I take the safe way," he explained. And yet, in spite of this, he has been caught by the *Brigade Touristique* many times. The first time he was set free with only a warning. The second time, and every time thereafter, he has served time in *al habs*. Surviving in jail, said the Lynx (sounding much like Driss the weaver), requires patience, *al sabr*, for without it one becomes "insane," or even "a real criminal." Jail, he tells me, can even be a positive experience. Once, a hard-timer inside tested the Lynx by crushing his hand with a heavy stone. The Lynx managed to maintain the outward appearance of calm, and by doing so was able to prevent further problems. After this the hard-timer told the guards, "just give me his two months and let this one go." The Lynx had earned respect. In fact, he tells me, "Jail is good." When I express my incredulity, he adds, "for homosexuals." If one has money, roughly 100 *dirhams* per day, "each day it is like sitting at a café on the outside." Ten times that amount can buy one better food, access to a toilet (not just a bucket in a common room), or fresh water, depending upon one's needs.

In answer to my questions about his perception of the Moroccan monarchy, the Lynx grew irritated. "Tourists know only one Moroccan, King Hassan II. They don't know there are twenty-four million Moroccans *living* underdevelopment (his emphasis)." "The king is a son of Morocco but doesn't *know* Moroccans (again, his emphasis))." "In Morocco you should live like a donkey, smiling all the time."

The Lynx met Al Malik through guiding, and is very proud[49] of the fact that he was earning money at it before Al Malik began to guide. After Al Malik opened his shop the Lynx worked exclusively for him. He knew plenty of others for whom he could have worked if he chose to, but the Lynx saw advantages for himself with Al Malik that the others could not match. While he remained vague about just what those advantages might be, I suspect that the Lynx appreciated Al Malik because, unlike other entrepreneurs engaged in selling to tourists, Al Malik was not only quite intelligent and, like the Lynx, able to grasp abstractions, but also he deferred to the Lynx's judgment, and respected the Lynx for his abilities.

According to the Lynx, cigarettes and smoking are absolutely necessary for protection, advice, and definition of self. "I smoke to move," he says. Like a key to the world, smoking has many functions for the Lynx. One smokes "to keep quiet." Or "to know yourself as a Moroccan." And "to make life." Without smoking, life is impossible.

I asked him about his notion of the future. He told me he wants a "serious" job someday. "I know bus time, bank time (by this he meant 'schedules' and 'business hours'), but I have never traveled and have no bank accounts." He has met the bus from Tétouan faithfully for twelve years, offering his services to arriving tourists. Those who come to Fez from Tétouan are often already suspicious and unwilling to trust approaching guides. "Tétouan takes people for smoke." That is, Europeans who are primarily interested in obtaining hashish get it in Tétouan, not elsewhere.[50] They are told, "You are a lucky man. Today is market day. You will get the best price." This is, of course, a lie. The guides assume that tourists who arrive in Fez are already suspicious, having run the gauntlet of

---

[49] Here the Lynx used the word "*unsuri*" referring to guiding being of elemental, constitutive importance to his definition of self.

[50] The Sharks generally buy their hashish from connections elsewhere in the Rif, if they are buying to resell it. The growers generally do not sell their product in quantities smaller than one kilo (cf. McMurry, 2001; McNeil, 1992).

hustlers in Tangiers, Tétouan, or Casablanca. Trust, therefore, must be won with care. The Lynx begins by explaining that he knows the trouble they have experienced, and that here, in Fez with him, it will be different. By taking "the safe way" the Lynx succeeds where others do not because he does not become aggressive. He uses patience and remains calm. Surprisingly often, tourists trust him, particularly since his presentation of self is in such contrast to that of other guides clamoring for a tourist's attention. "Before, tourists had things to trade, they were happy to talk, only to talk and meet people. Not like today. Now it is all money, money, money."

When his great-grandfather died he left behind only a drum. The Lynx told me that he is "following the *tambour* (drum)." He thinks of the drum as his coat-of-arms. It is a symbol of his independence, autonomy, and pride. In reference to my comments about the inherent difficulties of "the guiding way"—uncertain income, police repression, arrogant and insulting clients—he replied simply that "I know my life is fucked up. I do it [guiding] for fun." Then later he added, "Without problems, life would not be so sweet." In short, sadness makes life sweet according to the Lynx.

CHAPTER 15

Al Malik

> *Research literature in delinquency, social psychology, and child developmental psychology leaves little doubt about the causes of maladjustment and delinquency in preschool children through high school teenagers. Determinants for childhood disorders that lead to academic failure and to rejection by peers and teachers, as well as to the formation of delinquent groups and street gangs, are ineffective parenting and disturbed family social interactions. These determinants increase the risk for childhood depression, which then heightens the risk for involvement with a delinquent group.*
>
> —Fleisher (1995:112)

Al Malik is one of the undisputed survivors in Fez's "carpet wars"[51] for tourists' money. He has a stable of roughly thirty guides and is known by many more, as well as by other merchants. He has a very wide network of acquaintances. Some are "*'adu*" (enemies) while others are equals, or dependents—clients. Al Malik knows manufacturers of leather goods like Karim, who is, like Al Malik, in the business of selling, but Karim's primary market is Moroccan, not foreign tourists. Moroccans consume leather goods as fashionable high-status garments associated with contemporary lifestyles as opposed to traditional life-ways. This is ironic, given

---

[51]This is my term for the competition for tourodollars that occurs between guides and their patrons.

that it is precisely the folk tradition in carpets and leather goods, etc., that wealthy foreign tourists often want to buy. In theoretical terms, post-moderns seeking the authenticity of traditional handicraft goods meet aspiring moderns in the ancient ritual arena of the bazaar.

Al Malik's father was 85 when Al Malik was born in 1959. Eight elder siblings from his father's other wives were his mother's age when he was born (roughly twenty years older than Al Malik). He started at the Bab al Guissa Koranic School when he was four years old. After three years there he entered the primary school near Bab al Guissa (one of the ancient gates to the medina). At age twelve he went to the local "*collège*" (equivalent to an American junior high school) with every intention of being a model student. He was—and remains—bright and ambitious, though his ambitions are somewhat diminished now that the life he has led has worn him down and circumscribed his opportunities. His intellect remains vibrant, but perceptibly dulled by alcohol, hashish, and limited education. "I wanted to study," he says, but "at fourteen or fifteen I felt myself becoming a man." In short, he began to rebel. He was powerfully attracted to the possibilities of earning money by guiding tourists, and generally wanted to thumb his nose at the strict conformity of Moroccan pedagogy. He failed his third year and was forced to repeat it. He was entirely uninspired by the material being taught due to his increasing fascination with the guiding life: autonomy, nonconformity, and easy money. By 1973 many French tourists began to appear in Fez. By this time Al Malik could speak French well although he never learned to write it. "They [teachers and tourists] try to speak to me, I try to fuck them." By "speak" Al Malik means more than mere communication; it implies understanding, mutual goodwill, and respect. When he says that he tries to "fuck" them, he means that he tries to take advantage of them. For Al Malik, every relationship is conceived in terms of an economy of emotional or material "limited good": more for you equals less for me, therefore I will treat every interaction as a negotiation, one in which I will do all in my power to gain some benefit at your expense.

In fact, the guides have a common expression to describe this very aspect of their work: "*manny fik!*" The literal translation is, "my sperm in you!" But if uttered correctly, it sounds exactly like the

French exclamation, *"magnifique!"* For the guides, this pun provides endless hilarity. To the outsider the guide can appear to be echoing the praise for an item or experience, while among the guides themselves the implication is quite blunt and disdainful, "fuck you!"

By Al Malik's fourth year at *"collège"* he was in open rebellion against his teacher. "He tried to kill us," said Al Malik, by which he meant his teacher tried to break Al Malik's spirit. Their antagonism was very public and mutual. Al Malik was no longer interested in the virtues of studiousness and conformity. He repeated his fourth year with the same teacher.

It is at this point that Al Malik describes his life as "getting crazy." He went to school *"seulement pour faire la merde"* (only to cause problems, shit). "I thought of studying in the street." He traveled with foreign tourists "to learn their life," and to seduce European women. Although he was attracted to Europeans and their carefree lifestyles while on holiday, he rejected several opportunities to visit Europe. "Life here [in Morocco] is easier." Al Malik officially quit school at age 19, in 1979, and spent the next three years guiding tourists, learning as much as he could about guiding and selling.

During this period he earned his nickname, "Coco," the lunatic. He was widely recognized as someone who did not care about anything, especially his own person. Like the Animal, he was quite willing to use intimidation and violence, verbal and physical, to get his way. He soon became a well-known troublemaker. He formed a partnership with three friends and they opened their own shop, each putting up roughly $1000. Two were guides and two worked the shop. After a while disagreements caused Al Malik to pull out and for $1700 he opened his own shop. He made very little money at first because he "invested" in his friends. He paid higher commissions than other shop owners thereby attracting more business and making more contacts for his own patron-client network. "After about a year I began to make real money."

Al Malik has moved his operations several times, expanding his business and his influence with each move. Even though package tour groups generally do not make his venue a stop on their itineraries because it is too small and too far off the beaten track,[52] everyone who is anyone in Fez's tourist trade knows, or at least knows of, Al Malik.

---

[52] Also, Al Malik is not sophisticated enough to control himself for the sake of increased business. As his nickname implies, he is unpredictable. When I left Fez in 1994 Al Malik was convinced that if only he had a sign to advertise his shop, he would enjoy greater success. I suspect that greater success will elude him, and those like him, as well as the Sharks, as long as "retrograde" Islam remains a significant political force in Morocco.

CHAPTER 16

The Context of Suspicion

You tell me you are going to Fez.
Now, if you say you are going to Fez,
That means you are not going.
But I happen to know that you are going to Fez.
Why have you lied to me, you who are my friend?

—MOROCCAN PROVERB

One evening I was sitting with Al Malik and the others when the Lynx showed up with a tourist—a Frenchman employed by the railroad (*la Société Nationale des Chemin de Fers*) out of Marseilles, whom I will call Laurent. It was unusually late for tourists. The Lynx explained in Arabic that this guy had been to Fez several times before and was especially interested in a particular kind of carpet. The crew swung into action, showing Laurent their best examples of what he said he liked. He chose one and bought it. After the tension of the sale was dissipated by smiles and handshakes all around, a joint was produced, tea ordered, and Laurent was allowed to relax somewhat. I asked him in French how he came to find himself in Fez at such an hour of the night, and was he not a little scared to be out and about after nightfall? "Oh no," he assured me. "I feel quite safe."

At this, the assembled group of guides laughed uproariously. Pointing at me, they asked him, "Have you any idea who you're sitting next to?" Laurent looked mildly irritated and answered, no, why should he care? "Because," Al Malik replied, "he's only the most notorious Berber smuggler in Fez..." Laurent was noticeably unnerved and began to eye me suspiciously. Indeed, I was just as surprised as he was to learn of my alleged identity. Enjoying the joke, I played along, inventing various outrageous exploits and speaking in *Dérija* with the guides. I was only asking them if my tall tales were sufficient, but Laurent did not know this, for he could not speak more than a few words of Arabic.

When it became obvious that Laurent was no longer quite as comfortable as he had said he felt earlier, I decided to stop joking and allay his fears. "Actually," I told him in French, "I'm an American studying Anthropology and learning about the guides' way of life." Laurent was incredulous. "*Ah bon*?" "Yes, yes," I assured him. And to prove it, I produced what to me was the ultimate of all *bona fides*, my American passport.

Laurent examined it and seemed satisfied. He held it up so the assembled pranksters could see. This only caused further hilarity.

"You believe *him*?!" Al Malik sneered. "That document is a forgery! Anyone can buy one for $200 here in the medina…"

At this, Laurent quickly returned my passport, as if to hold it might implicate him in some dangerous adventure well beyond the manageable excitement that the Lynx had provided by guiding him to Al Malik's shop so late in the evening, so deep in the old city. Nothing I could say or do would have changed Laurent's mind after that. Al Malik and the others had made a Berber smuggler of me and that was that.

In a different context, as the holder of an American passport, I could do things that ordinary Moroccans could not. For example, one night while walking home, I came out of the *Mellah* by a different route for a change, and instead of staying on the sidewalk, I cut across the wide plaza in front of the Royal Palace gates. During the day this is a pleasant place to walk: it offers clear, unobstructed passage, wide-open space so rare in the medina, as well as luxuriant greenery, and a fountain—all far from the belching fumes of passing lorries on the road leading past the gates to the palace and the old city. Guides will, on occasion, try for tourists here, although the pickings are rarely interesting compared to other spots, especially the Blue Gate, *Bab Boujeloud*, where many tours begin. At night the plaza is eerily quiet, and absolutely deserted. Or so it would seem.

As I began to cross, out of the shadows emerged two armed palace guards. They shouted at me in *Dérija*, "*Aji, aji!*" (Come here!), and were clearly intent upon impeding my passage, and possibly making my life unpleasant as well. I told them politely in Arabic that I was an American and they smiled, certain that I was lying. When I produced the magical blue passport clearly stamped with "The United States of America" they looked confused. "*Ma yumkinsh...*" (not possible) muttered one to the other. "*Yumkin,*" (possible) I replied, and produced, in addition to the passport, my "*Certificat d'Immatriculation*" signed by *le Directeur Général de la Sûreté Nationale*—the Moroccan State Police. Suddenly the two guards were ecstatic: a real, live American! With them! Right here! All smiles and declarations of friendship, one said to me in English, "We are all like brothers!" The other one added, "America is good!" They escorted me to the other end of the plaza and waved me on with cheerful goodwill, very different indeed from their initial mien. I felt very fortunate to be held in such high regard, for I had seen these two guards behave quite differently toward my Moroccan friends on a number of other occasions.

CHAPTER 17

Learning to be Useful

Ils mentent comme ils soufflent. ("They lie like they breathe.")

—Francophone Moroccan Saying

One afternoon at Al Malik's shop, a guide named Burweis[53] bounded up the narrow stairway into the showroom at Al Malik's at the head of a rather large (for this time of day and at this point in the season) group of tourists from America. He appeared agitated, his face red; clearly he was worried about something. "*Schnoo?*" (what?) Al Malik asked while Sidi Zitoun smirked all-knowingly in the corner. "A large group of tourists from [and here he shot me a sidelong glance] America..." He quickly exchanged words I could not hear with Al Malik, then after Al Malik deliberated momentarily and had given his assent, Burweis asked me if I would help him. Happily, I told him, I would do whatever I could.

It turned out that he needed me to convince these Americans to buy from Al Malik. "How?" I asked. After more words with Al Malik and again, his quick nod of assent to Little Head, I was let in on the scheme. Sidi Zitoun was already welcoming the eleven tourists into the larger showroom, showing them the loom where Driss ordinarily would have been working. Unfortunately he was not there weaving the "Berber blankets" Al Malik specialized in, for it was after quitting time (his presence mesmerizes and helps grease the squeaky wheels of commerce in tourodollars). I could hear Sidi Zitoun

---

[53]*Burweis* means "little head"; they call him this because he is not quick-thinking like most of the others, but it is also a not-so-veiled reference to his penis.

intoning the ritual greetings for Anglophones, "*Marhababikum...* Welcome, welcome, you are welcome. Please relax, sit down, sit down..." It was curious to me how the more he tried to make some people feel welcome or comfortable, the more they felt uncomfortable and nervous.

Little Head had told them that he was Al Malik's cousin, on the assumption that family connections are more trustworthy: the tourists could trust Little Head and therefore, by extension, be sure of getting good deals at his cousin Al Malik's shop. Further, making matters more complex, Little Head had told them that I, an American no less, came regularly to buy from Al Malik, adding another layer of legitimacy to his story. "Go, tell them to buy from Al Malik," Little Head ordered me. Off I went.

It was clear that these people were very nervous, they laughed the short "ha-ha-ha" of discomfiture, and smiled the quick, thin smiles that typically denote formality, not conviviality, and so I tried to be as genuinely friendly as I could in an effort to relax the atmosphere. This proved to be impossible. The venue was altogether too foreign and the Americans were very much on guard, expecting to be taken advantage of at any moment. I asked where they were from—Wisconsin. I tried to engage in conversation—only monosyllabic answers were the result. I told them that I was a regular customer, that they could have confidence in their guide, Little Head, that this was a very honest and forthright family business... All lies, and they saw right through me. Yet, nevertheless, several did express interest in the least expensive "Berber blankets" that Sidi Zitoun showed them. I stood aside while he bargained with the interested parties. He sold three.

"Your sales pitch needs work," Little Head said to me after the group left, not having bought as much as he had hoped. I had thought it was a minor victory that anything had been sold at all.

CHAPTER 18

Working for the Lynx

The bargain-hunter goes delightfully mad in these endless souks. Tourist trash or the real thing, it makes no great difference in the everlasting memory of this first vision of an Oriental bazaar. The sheen of scarves, the gleam of beaten copper and the twinkle of brass, the vibrant dyes of leather-goods tooled in gold, the confusion of color and sound and the scenters of mint and musk—surely, there could be no more thrilling a beginning to a trip across North Africa than this dive into a maelstrom of Arabian Night's delights.

—HULME (1930:24)

One morning after I had been in Fez for some time, I went down to *Bab Boujeloud*, the main point of entry to Fez al-Bali for tourists, and the Lynx ran up to me and breathlessly asked what my plans for the morning were. I had none in particular I told him. "Good," he said. "Today you will work with me." I was elated. At last an opportunity to see for myself what guiding was really like. The Lynx told me that the police were arresting guides down near the central mosque, a popular tourist destination.[54] He wanted me to lead his tour of about twelve Britons through that part of town and meet him on the other side of the tanneries, where it was safe from

---

[54] The *Brigade Touristique* of Fez's police force was, at the time, short-staffed for their task of controlling the unlicensed guides, but what they lacked in numbers they made up for in cruelty. Because so few officers chased so many guides, the latter could count on the former being only in certain places, the locations of which an informal network of "friendlies" would note and pass the word.

police patrols and interference. The Lynx then took me to the café where he had installed his flock and introduced me as his "American friend."

I tagged along through *Bab Boujeloud*, past the trinket hawkers and through the tunnel-like meat and vegetable market with its colorful sights and smells, all the way to the *Madrasa Bou Inania* where the Lynx peeled off, leaving me to lead the group. I later asked the Lynx why he chose this particular place to leave us. He said it was simply a convenient opportunity. He also told me that he assumed I would know more about its history than did he since I often ducked inside to sit in a sunny corner and rest. According to the Fez Tourism Bureau, the *madrasa*

> was built between 1350 and 1357 by Sultan Abou Inan and was the last one built by the Merinids. It is extremely big and displays many typical signs of Merinid architecture (such as bronze, marble, and onyx decoration; cedar woodwork; and windows with overhanging stalactites). This madrasa is currently the only religious building in Morocco open to non-Moslems.

It is indeed a pleasant place, for within its walls the noise and bustle of Fez is muffled and one hears the gentle susurration of the fountain in the courtyard and the cooing of pigeons. The *zelige* tilework is stunning: Koranic verses in Kufic and Thuluth scripts ring the courtyard at eye level in brilliant blue on white. Below the verses a complex geometrical pattern continues to the floor, itself a checkerboard pattern of tiles, all blue and white. The overall effect is impressive.

Having already spoken with tanners at one of the smaller tanneries near the *Boujeloud* gate, marveled at the open air market, and savored the exoticism and titillations of orientalist myth at the top of the *Talaa Kebira*, I led the Britons down, deeper into the old city.[55] As we wound our way into the depths of the medina, I paused

---

[55] From among the myriad descriptions of Fez, the following example serves nicely to illustrate the accreted layers of expectation that have built up around the experience of entering the old city. "First knocked nearly off one's legs by a passing camel, then picked up on the other side by a blow from a donkey's pannier, one fights one's way along, here jammed into a corner with a hideous old hag, who hastily covers her face lest the infidel should behold her charms; then carried forward with the crowd, who are eager to kiss the garment

occasionally to point out certain features and sites I found especially picturesque or interesting, such as a colorfully tiled fountain, or Maimonides' house[56]. I picked a route that meandered somewhat, an excellent way of getting my charges disoriented and "lost" in the disorderly streets of Fez's medina, thus allowing them to feel truly outside of their known universe and in the realm of mysterious expectation and enchantment that is so much a part of Fez's allure.

I knew the city and wanted the Lynx's tourists to know that I knew it. I made use of the simple ruses the guides rely upon to cause maximum *dépaysement* such as taking indirect routes through the narrowest passages. This serves to make the tourists all the more vulnerable and reliant upon their guide.

We retraced a route that Sidi Zitoun had shown me several weeks earlier. It diverged from the main thoroughfare and took us through a covered alleyway only two meters wide, a dim tunnel really. Then, unexpectedly, we ducked through a very low doorway (roughly 1.5 meters square) and into a much smaller, narrower tunnel. The real Fez! Totally strange and most certainly not on the beaten track or in any guidebook. Another low doorway off of this

---

of the great man who is ambling by on his mule; at one moment side by side with a respectable merchant, the next jostling with a grinning idiot, stark naked, a mass of vermin, sores and filth, who is quite likely as not to tear one to pieces with his teeth, while the crowd looks on and approves. Side by side by one are dirty, barefoot Jews, obsequious and cringing; strange, half savage creatures from the mountains; good humored looking negro slaves; and beggars maimed, halt and blind, one stumbles, and, picking oneself up, amidst a perfect cloud of flies, discovers the half putrid carcass of a donkey has caused the fall..." Major General H. E. Colville, *A Ride in Petticoats and Slippers* (1884:141).

[56]"Moses Maimonides (Rabbi Moshe ben Maimon, usually referred to in Hebrew by the acronym 'RaMBa'M') was one of the towering figures in medieval intellectual and religious life. In addition to his law code, he excelled in the fields of philosophy, science, medicine, exegesis and communal leadership. Though born in Spain, in his youth his family fled religious persecution, [spending several years in Fez] settling in Egypt. Maimonides' literary output includes: a work on philosophical logic; an Arabic commentary to the Mishnah; an enumeration of the 613 precepts of the Torah; the *Mishneh Torah* law code; the Arabic philosophical treatise *The Guide of the Perplexed*; and many letters and *response* addressed to various Jewish communities" (Segal:1981).

dark alleyway gives access to the small workshop of a smelter, an artisan who makes and repairs teapots. A hand-bellows showered sparks and added orange fire-glow to the dim light of a single exposed bulb hanging from the unevenly timbered ceiling. The main effect of this detour was to make the ordinary stuff of culture, streets, and utensil repair appear more exotic than it otherwise would be if seen in *al jutaya*, for instance.

I let my group gawk a while as I chatted about this and that with the workmen there in the gloom. On behalf of my tourists, I asked the Moroccans if they would like to earn a few coins by letting the Britons take each other's photograph in the medieval-seeming workshop among the sooty, smiling, bright-eyed men. A few flash-bulbs popped and coins jingled between pockets and hands, and we were off again, down the narrow tunnel that soon led into an even narrower canyon whose walls tilted at strange angles, almost as if collapsing onto each other. The morning sky was a thin ribbon far above our heads.

The route jogs around a few bends, past other doorways to other workshops and homes, out of which the occasional housemaid would appear only to dart back inside with a giggle when she noticed the gaggle of tourists, with me at the front speaking English and an accented *Dérijah*. "*Sba al khair*," (good morning) I say politely as we pass.

This route is particularly good because it loops around and intersects with the *Talaa Kebira* again just above the restaurant *Palais Mérinides*, a 14th century palace that has been restored and made into a tourist attraction. I had met the manager by way of an introduction from some of the neighborhood's guides, and had naively managed to leave the impression that I would bring any clients I could to him. In exchange for my solicitude for his wellbeing, he was graciously willing to permit me the occasional use of his toilet, one of the few western-style flush toilets in that part of the old city. (Though seemingly a trivial matter, the plumbing of Fez's medina can not generally accommodate *papier hygenique*. Therefore the vast majority of facilities consist of nothing but a hole and a spigot for rinsing oneself and one's left hand. Cholera outbreaks are not uncommon in Fez.)

I led my group to his restaurant where he proudly showed them the tile fountain in the central covered courtyard of the palace, now the dining room of his establishment specializing in "authentic Moroccan cuisine." It was a stereotypical example of twisting local culture to fit the expectations of visiting Western "others." The group was impressed with the ornate tile work on the floors, the carved plaster and cedar ceilings, and the carpets hanging from the railings of second and third-story balconies high above our heads. It was, however, too early for lunch, so rather than insisting we stay for a meal, the manager let us go with what seemed like genuine friendliness, seeing us to the door and saying in carefully rehearsed English "You are welcome in Fez," bidding the Britons to enjoy their visit.

I knew, however, that he was upset with me for not timing our arrival better, and I felt ashamed: I should have planned the tour more carefully to coincide with the pangs of hunger that a long walk in the old city can produce. All I could say to him was, "*Mara ahora, inchalla... Smahili*" (next time, Allah willing... Excuse me). I also knew that these tourists were not likely to spend much money. They had told me so beforehand. Yet it was axiomatic among the guides never to believe such claims from tourists. I was a curious double-agent. The Britons had to trust me; to rely upon me, to a certain degree, while I traded on my Western status to get information. I then tried to use that status and information for the benefit of the guides and those whom they "fed" with customers in turn. But, clearly, I had failed miserably. My relationship with the manager of the *Palais Mérinides* had been damaged by my failure to supply him with customers. As we left I caught myself worrying about whether or not he would be willing to let me use his toilet again.

From the *Palais*, I led the group back to the *Talaa Kebira*, on past the leather goods hanging outside small shops, down through dank, narrow passages that twisted and turned, all contributing to the feeling that one was well beyond the borders of "Christendom." We passed neighborhood bakeries where children and their mothers, or Berber maids, brought dough to be baked into the chewy disk-shaped loaves distinctive to this part of Morocco. Private homes in Fès al-Bali rarely had their own ovens and therefore relied upon the communal bakeries for their daily bread.

On we went, past other neighborhood institutions, such as the public baths (*al hammam*) where, for a few coins, one could scrub and steam off the grime of the city and emerge perfumed and gloriously refreshed.

Finally the cobblestones leveled off and we were in the central market district, the *"kissaria,"* a covered area perhaps the size of a city block or two, and packed with merchants selling the leather slippers, *"balrha"* for which Fez is famous (yellow is the traditional color, but they come in every conceivable hue). Silks, too, are to be found in every shade, as well as bolts of other cloth (wool and cotton, mostly), candles, gold brocade belts, framed velvet embroidered with phrases from the Qu'ran, spices, henna, dates and nuts, candies, couscous steamers, household utensils, hardware, and an apparently endless variety of other goods ranging from locally produced *artisinat* to imported shoes and Chicago Bulls athletic clothing. Here the labyrinth becomes more rectilinear, for the central market district burned down in the 1960's and has been rebuilt along more "rational" lines. It is not spacious, however, and the crowds are like streams of cattle being herded through chutes. There are veritable currents and tides of people shouting prices, haggling, or arguing over politics and generally engaging in the time-honored activities associated with the bazaar.

In an effort to avoid the thickest crush of shoppers, I led my tourists through a detour by way of the tailors' *souk*. It is calmer because fewer people shop here. The tailors were making the quintessentially Moroccan hooded gowns called *djellaba*. The tailors sew by hand, seated cross-legged on pillows in small stalls at waist height. They are assisted by young boys, apprentices, who can often be seen holding long taut loops of thread, one in each finger, and quickly switching them back and forth, from hand to hand as the tailor himself embroiders an elaborate series of small knotted buttons and loops at the throat of the *djellaba*, as well as an equally elaborate design on the cuffs and edge of the hood. It is the quality of cloth and of the embroidery that distinguishes a proper *djellaba al-Fassie* from others of humbler origins.

The group of Britons appreciated the slower pace, finding it a great relief from the thronging crowds and sometimes frightening press of people and beasts of burden composing the quotidian norm of Fès al-Bali's *souks*. They "ooohed" and "aaahed," admiring the patience of the tailors, who for the most part ignored their obsequious smiles. Several of the tailors specifically requested me not to allow photographs when one of the tourists pulled out a camera. I obliged, explaining that they were too modest, when in fact I suspect they were just basically annoyed. Several of the tourists asked if the young boys were not supposed to be in school. I responded by saying that the boys were in fact "in school" learning the art and work of producing the hand-made *djellaba*.

I cajoled one tailor whom I knew to allow a few photos to be taken of himself and his work. He obliged me, glad of an opportunity to earn a few coins and also, in part, to take advantage of the occasion to irritate the other tailors who had been unnecessarily gruff toward me the first time I had shown up asking in halting Arabic for a *djellaba* of my own. He had made a thick, warm *djellaba* for me to wear when winter descended upon the Sais Plain and Fez grew cold and grey. I wore it regularly. In it I felt anonymous and free from the aggressive glares that often greet outsiders.[57] When first we met, before he would do business with me, the tailor insisted that I recite the *ashahadu*.[58] I did and he was satisfied. Younger than the others, he had less to lose in the prestige hierarchy among the tailors of that *souk*, than they by dealing with me, an outsider. I wanted to show him that that I appreciated his openness toward me, so I hoped that by bringing these tourists to him he might be able to make some money.

One of the tourists, I will call him Paul, decided he would like to entertain the idea of obtaining a *djellaba* of his own. Indeed, it is possible, I told him. It could be sent on to him, or he could return to collect it in a week, perhaps after visiting other places in Morocco. He agreed and decided to purchase one. Measuring him for the garment became a festive interlude for all the tailors in that *souk*, for this fellow was well over six feet tall and towered over most other people in the entire country, much less a *Fassie souk*.

---

[57] A feeling, I suspect, which is similar to that provided by a woman's veil.

[58] "*Ashahadu an la ilaha ill Allah wa ashahadu anna Muhammadar Rasul Allah.*" This phrase is the shibboleth, utterance of which transforms the infidel into a Muslim. It means, "I witness there is no God but God, and Mohammed is his prophet."

His very presence fairly screamed *nisrani* ("outsider," "tourist"). He thus drew considerable attention wherever he went. To be in the *souk* of the tailors, suddenly an intimate place in a public space, in stark contrast to the hubbub of the madding crowds only a few meters away, was to Paul and the other tourists, disorienting. The tailors laughed at him not in derision, but rather in amusement at his bewilderment. It was a lighthearted break for the tourists and tailors alike.

All the Moroccans in the *souk* got involved it seemed. Some offered advice while others merely smirked. "A summer *djellaba*." "No, a *khamisse-sirwal*," the traditional baggy pants and ample shirt, a part of any Muslim man's wardrobe. "This cloth is the best for it is whitest!" "No, try my wool with the authentic Berber pattern!" Paul began to laugh with giddy nervousness at so much open solicitude where just moments before there had been only dour-faced resentment. Paul finally settled on a brown and white striped wool and cotton cool-weather *djellaba*. Measurements were concluded with efficiency (sleeves, shoulders' breadth and width, height from neck to ankles) and duly noted in the tailor's notebook.

I negotiated a price I thought was fair, based upon what I had been told by other Moroccans such a garment "ought to cost." Prices are never fixed, however, and depend on myriad circumstances and details beyond the objective costs and profit margins of the vendor. In Paul's case, I obtained a more-or-less "correct" or respectable price for the garment. I suggested that a reasonable tip of ten or fifteen percent would not offend these men. Satisfied with the arrangement that he would return in a week to collect his authentic *djellaba,* Paul happily paid roughly sixty-five dollars. A Moroccan from Fez would have paid two-thirds the price that I negotiated for Paul.

We left the tailors' *souk* and proceeded through the arcaded brick market. I led my procession of tourists past "the ice cream corner," whose vendor did a brisk business with my clients. He shared an inconspicuous conspiratorial wink with me, and handed me a cone *gratis* as he did so. It was better than *jabba*.

Ice cream in hand, we moved on into the date sellers' *souk* where we were forced to pause due to a stately, if noisy, parade celebrating a circumcision. When the knot of revelers had passed, we continued on and rounded a corner at which there is a small photography studio displaying photographs of women's hennaed hands, and found ourselves at the great *Al Quarawiyyine* mosque in the heart of Fès al-Bali.

I dutifully told the tourists what I knew about the great mosque[59]: that it accommodated up to twenty thousand worshippers at once, that it is the spiritual center of the city, perhaps of all Morocco, that green is the color of Islam and that is why the glazed tiles of the roof are such a brilliant shade of green, that beggars congregate at the main gates to the mosque to make their appeal for alms because it is the duty of pious Muslims to give to those less fortunate; and finally that in Morocco, it is forbidden to enter any mosque, especially this one, unless one is a Muslim.[60] The group gazed in wonder through the great iron gates at the immense courtyard of blue and white brilliantly glazed tiles, toward the massive fountain that occupies the center of the mosque's

---

[59] According to *The Dictionary of Islamic Architecture*: "The Qarawiyyin Mosque, founded in 859, is the most famous mosque of Morocco and attracted continuous investment by Muslim rulers. There were extensive renovations in 956 by the Umayyad caliph of Spain who also added the minaret. The building did not reach its present form and size (85 by 44 m) until 1135. The prayer hall comprises ten aisles running parallel to the *qibla* wall and a raised transverse aisle leading to the *mihrab*. The aisles are covered with gabled wooden roofs covered with roof tiles. There is a dome over the *mihrab* and the entrance porch in addition to the seven domes which cover the north arcade of the courtyard. The domes are made of elaborate *muqarnas* vaulting with zig-zag ribbing on the exterior. Inside the mosque is decorated with stucco, the most elaborate being reserved for the area in front of the *mihrab*. The mosque preserves its twelfth-century *minbar* which is regarded as one of the finest in the world. The courtyard is decorated with tile mosaic (*zilij*) dadoes and has a magnificent ablutions pavilion at the west. The pavilion, built in the sixteenth century, rests on eight marble columns and has a tile-covered wooden roof with overhanging eaves. The woodwork of the eaves is of exceptional quality with carved *muqarnas* mouldings and miniature engaged piers forming blind niches decorated with geometric interlace" (Petersen 1996).

[60] This is not the case in Egypt or Israel. In these two countries one may enter any mosque, regardless of one's religion—as long as men remove their shoes and women cover their heads.

vast courtyard. Several men were gathered around the rim of the fountain, performing their ritual ablutions in preparation for *al zuhar*, the noon prayer.

As we stood by, more and more people began to pass through the massive wooden doors at one of the portals to the sanctuary. Then the muezzin's call rang from the minaret, "*Allahu akbar! Allahu akbar! Allahu akbar!*" Other muezzins at other mosques could soon be heard echoing the call to prayer across the city. The crowds thinned as the faithful concluded the morning's affairs and paused to pray throughout the city. The tourists respectfully watched the *umma* gather in worship.

Suddenly, two plainclothes police officers from the *Brigade Touristique* appeared before me, blocking our path. Startled, I nonetheless managed to regain my composure and produced my American passport and *Carte d'Immitriculation*. It was their turn to be taken by surprise. After an awkward moment, they pretended to notice something absorbing in the other direction and moseyed off. I suggested we press on and make our way back to where the Lynx would be waiting.

I led the group on a twisting path through some of the most picturesque sections of the city between *Al Quarawiyyine* and *Funduk Yehudi*, passing along the way a small leather shop at which one of the women in our group noticed something she might like to buy. She and two of her friends began inspecting the goods more closely. This drew the attention of a young man nearby—not the shopkeeper—who immediately seized this as an opportunity to make some money. He offered his assistance and became belligerent when the offer was declined. The tourists pointed to me, indicating that I was their guide. In an effort to blunt his antagonism, I explained to the lad, I will call him Mohammed, that if he was softer in his approach, he could do better with some of the men who were clearly interested, yet also hesitant to let their desires be known for fear of the all-too-common high-pressure sales tactics. It is just this kind of pressure that has led many tourists and travelers to report that they will not return to Morocco. Thus, as Mohammed tried to allay the embarrassed Englishmen's fears, which had been exacerbated by Paul's earlier experience while purchasing his *djellaba*, I bargained with the shopkeeper on behalf of the two women who had decided that a leather handbag and vest were to be theirs.

The sale was concluded after arriving at what I felt was another respectable compromise on a price. One of the men decided he too wanted something, now confident of my abilities to obtain a fair deal. I helped him essentially by discussing the matter with Mohammed. How much did he need to make on the sale? I quoted a price to the English fellow that he seemed pleased with, enough so that he purchased the souvenir. After he paid, off we went to rejoin the Lynx.

A few moments later, Mohammed ran to catch me. He told me to let the others go on without me, I could catch up shortly. I explained to the group that they needed only to continue in the same direction and I would be with them directly. After the others were out of sight in the swelling crowds, he deftly palmed me a carefully folded 100 *dihram* note, roughly $9. It was my *jabba*, my "cut," from the sales at the leather shop.

I tried to refuse the money, but Mohammed insisted. Only minutes before he had been antagonistic and competitive. Now he was happily sharing the spoils with me. I gave him a laugh and we enjoyed our complicity in earning money so effortlessly. He adamantly refused to take any of what he had determined to be my share, suggesting that to do so would be dishonorable, unfair even. I thanked him as graciously as I could and, so as not to insult him, I pocketed the cash. Later I would spend it on the Lynx in "repayment" for his trust in me. I caught up with the tourists and explained that Mohammed had wanted merely to wish them well, sure that my lie would arouse suspicion. It did not.

I then led the group toward Al Malik's carpet shop where it would again be safe for the Lynx to resume control of his tour. We took a few turns and then climbed up the narrow, uneven stairs to Al Malik's shop where Driss the weaver was making blankets at his ancient loom with his assistant. Al Malik himself was across the alley in the café playing cards. Only Sidi Zitoun in his snappy sport coat and tie, and the much younger Muscles in his jeans and t-shirt, were there. They were showing cheap *zarbia* to a German couple who were clearly interested in moving on. Their guide smiled at me, and pretending to be tired of the carpet shop and concerned for his Germans, he told Sidi Zitoun that these two were not buyers today and that he would be back later. Al Malik soon showed up, after I had gotten everyone seated comfortably on the low benches ringing the room. Carpets hung from nails driven into the wooden joists at the ceiling, covered the walls, giving the rooms an intimate and insulated ambience.

"*Salaam aleikum*," intoned Al Malik. "Just looking?" he asked.

"Yes," all the Britons answered.

"It is good to look," Al Malik told them. He added his standard counter-argument to the tourists' protests as he ordered his assistants to begin showing carpets: "it costs nothing to look." Speaking in *Dérija* he told Muscles and Sidi Zitoun to start by showing only the mediocre pieces, nothing fancy yet.

A dazzling array of carpets were slowly unfurled at our feet. After three or four had been displayed (a show in itself, for they must be presented in a particular fashion, not simply strewn about), a small boy arrived carrying glasses of tea for each of the Britons, myself, and Al Malik (Sidi Zitoun, the Lynx and Muscles were saving their money). The boy was the café-owner's son and at first did not recognize me. He did a double take when he realized that I had been guiding for the Lynx. He then smiled the smile of complicity in some great game, knowing that if all went well he would be eating meat with Friday's *xixous* (Fassie couscous). The profits of a sale are distributed rather widely: everyone who has had a hand in selling an item of value will generally be compensated for their labor, as I had been after leaving the leather shop. As tea-bringer, the boy's share would be given to his father. While Sidi Zitoun and Muscles laid each successive rug over the one already on the floor, Al Malik would ask them to pause a moment, inviting the tourists to feel the material, to walk across them in bare feet, even to smell them.

"Can you smell the sheep from the Atlas?" he was fond of asking.

I could tell that several of the women in the group were no longer as nervous as they had seemed to be that morning. The men, however, remained wary. No rugs were sold, and eventually the

Lynx was forced to assume the same attitude as had the other guide, with the Germans, earlier. He left, suggesting to Al Malik that he would be back later. I wished the Britons a pleasant stay in Morocco, and remained in Al Malik's shop to enjoy my tea.

That evening the Lynx returned, and thanked me for my help. I refused his offer of *al jabba*, my share in the profits from his time with the Britons, whom he had installed at a campground near the outskirts of the city. Because the Lynx was more familiar with me, unlike the young Mohammed at the leather shop, he accepted my generosity without taking offence. He knew that I knew that he gave money to his uncle's household where he kept his few possessions and that, unlike me, he was of meager means. There was no shame in accepting gifts from me.

CHAPTER 19

Entranced

> *The energy of instincts is pure in the sense that it has no connotation of good or bad. The question of good and bad arises only when the social destiny of men is considered.*
>
> —MERNISSI (1987:1)

I was invited to Al Malik's brother's *usbu'a*, the naming ceremony and party held to celebrate the birth of a child. It was a very formal event. The *usbu'a* is important for a variety of reasons. The family had to demonstrate its traditional importance within the neighborhood (*huma*). As a family of a 400-year recorded lineage in Fez, Al Malik's brother was obliged to go into debt to provide a ceremony worthy of their elite pretensions. There was a videographer which is *de rigeur*, and as a great honor to me, I was asked to be the photographer. I was delighted to accept.

On the appointed evening, at roughly seven, I presented myself in my best suit, my shoes polished, my hair cut, my pockets loaded with film, my camera at the ready. I recognized only a few people in the crowd, which numbered over one hundred. An orchestra was playing beautiful *Aïssawa* music in the courtyard of the palace that had been rented for the occasion.[61] Six large tables were

---

[61]The ritual of *Aïssawa* actually includes six phases: *al hizb, al dhikr, al horm, al haddun, al hadra*, and finally *al dhikroullah*. The instruments associated with *Aïssawa* are single-membrane tambourines, double-membrane drums, oboes, and in Sidi Said Berrada's orchestra, long *basso profundo* trumpets.

arranged in the courtyard, opposite the orchestra. There were too many people for the available tables so the guests ate in shifts. First came the most important males, then the more peripheral males, next the important women, after which the least important women and the young children took their turns at the low tables and banquettes. It was a sumptuous repast indeed: exquisite *petit plats* followed by four main courses of chicken, lamb, fish, and *bastila* (pigeon pie, a specialty of Fez). Overpoweringly sweet desserts too numerous to list completed the meal, followed by coffee and mint tea.

I ate, paying my respects to the family's honor and praising them for their lavish generosity as was expected, while making polite conversation with my neighbors. When we finished, I excused myself and headed toward the door, ducking into the dark, narrow tunnel that led to the street. I needed some fresh air, or at least what passes for it in the medina. Outside I found Al Malik and several others, including his uncle who is a detective with the local constabulary. They were discussing the party so far. The others offered criticisms to tease Al Malik and his brother. "The food was bad," said one. "Too little," said another. "And the women in your family are not at all attractive," said a third with a mock sneer. Indeed, there were some who were quite striking. One, I noticed, had been staring at me disconcertingly as I ate. This was to have dire, and totally unanticipated, consequences.

All the while the music had been drifting throughout the palace and spilling into the *huma*. Sidi Said Berrada and his *Aïssawa* orchestra were beginning to affect the audience. I was totally unprepared for what happened next.

Aïssawa is trance music. It is the music of Moroccan Sufism, originating in the 16th century from the *zaouia* of Sidi Mohamed Ben Aïssa in Meknès. According to legend, when the *marabout* died in 1526, one of his followers was so overcome with grief that he became entranced, tearing his clothes, and mutilating his body. Perhaps to emphasize the totality of his transformation, he is described as having proceeded to eat a sheep and a goat—raw. Through the centuries, the worship of this saint achieved acceptance and an orthodoxy of sorts. The Sufi adepts devote themselves to asceticism and ecstatic communion with the divine through music based upon *dhikr*, the repetition of praises to the prophet and Allah. The singing combined with the music ideally produces *hadra*, or ecstatic trance.

I was enjoying the music, swaying to its rhythm. It was late in the evening and I was tired, though no one in the courtyard around me showed the slightest signs of fatigue, nor gave the least suggestion of preparing to leave. Glancing around me, I noticed an elderly woman rise to her feet and begin to sway back and forth. She moved ponderously and slowly at first, but in no time she was gaining speed and growing increasingly frenzied with her arms flailing and her head whipping about. Other women began to behave in similar fashion, rising to their feet and becoming carried away by the music. With each new dancer, Sidi Berrada seemed to gain more energy and sang with greater power and urgency, all the while backed by the surging power of the music. As the women became ever more oblivious of the audience at their feet, young men rose and hovered behind the women, arms outstretched, protecting them from their own exuberance.

After the final *dikhroullah* the *usbu'a* broke up and I was invited to spend what remained of the night with Al Malik's mother's family. I was shown a room with space on one of the low banquettes, given a blanket, and fell into a deep yet fitful sleep.

The next day I went to have the film developed. I waited eagerly for the prints. I was looking forward to sharing them with Al Malik before offering them to his brother. The photographs would be a symbol of my gratitude for their generosity, and of my goodwill toward Al Malik and his family. They would simultaneously remind them of the *usbu'a* and of me, their good friend from America.

To my horror the film was ruined. Every frame of every roll was overexposed. Upon close inspection I determined that my camera was broken. A minute crack where the lens attached to the body had been allowing light onto the film. I was devastated.

When I told Al Malik what had happened he just shrugged, as if to say "I expected as much from the likes of you."

CHAPTER 20

Unraveling

> *"In a situation where there was everything to be gained by agreement and friendliness there could be nothing but suspicion, hostility and bickering. It was always that way; it would go on being that way."*
>
> —BOWLES (1955:67)

After seven months in Fez, I decided to take a short break from the stress of living in the guides' world and made plans to visit my parents in New England. When I mentioned this to Al Malik he asked me to take four kilim carpets with me and sell them in America for him. He also wanted me to get him a pair of Teva sandals he had noticed tourists sporting of late. He admired them, and the versions available in Morocco were cheap imitations. I agreed. In retrospect, this was a serious mistake.

Upon reaching my parents' home in western Massachusetts I made inquiries at the local boutiques that ordinarily dealt in "ethnic" imported goods. None were interested in my wares. It became increasingly clear that outside of the setting of Fez's medina, these carpets lost much of their attractiveness. Eventually, friends bought the carpets, but I did not drive a hard bargain. After all, they were doing me a favor. I purchased a pair of sandals for Al Malik with some of the money.

Upon my return to Fez I proudly presented them to him, along with the rest of the money from the sales of the four kilims. At first, Al Malik looked puzzled. Then he grew angry. The sum I gave him was hardly more than his cost! The sandals constituted a scandalously meager profit. Al Malik waited until we were alone, out of respect for our reputations, before he told me that he had thought that by letting me sell carpets for him, the example of a *nisrani* actually helping a Muslim would become a reality. But no. I had betrayed him. He declared that he would not wear the sandals. He gave them away to a cousin who happily showed them off, antagonizing me by doing so, for I felt simply awful about the whole matter. I had wanted to help Al Malik, but had realized I could not ask my friends in New England to pay what I knew was an unfair, inflated price for merchandise that was not particularly to their taste. This was the beginning of escalating difficulties between me and Al Malik that was later to erupt into anger, bitterness, and recrimination.

I had been having other problems with Al Malik as well. He was angered by the fact that he had learned that I had paid the Lynx and his partner for granting me an extended interview. He felt that I should have paid him too, after everything he had told me. If I were to pay anyone, it should have been him. He was also insulted because I had gone to another source for information. Finally, he was angry with me for not having told him I was going to interview the Lynx.

All of this came out in a heated late evening discussion in the back room of a café at *Bab Boujeloud*. I had arranged to meet with Al Malik and Little Head. They looked grim, refusing to let me buy the tea. Al Malik began by telling me that he knew I had been talking to the Lynx. "How?" I stupidly asked. He brushed my question aside. "*Mish mohim*," (it's not important) he told me. What was important was that I now pay *him*. "How much?" "*Elfain doolar*" (two thousand dollars). "That's impossible, and even if I could pay it I would never do it." I went on to explain that I felt I needed to pay the Lynx because by talking to me he was losing the opportunity to earn revenue by working instead of "wasting" a day answering my questions. He could have been out hustling tourists. I paid him what he would have earned had he been guiding, a reasonable solution for us both. I pointed out that when I spoke with Al Malik I was always careful not to interrupt his sales efforts. I engaged him in conversation only when there were no customers in his shop. So I had not, in my opinion, interfered with his business. This explanation did not sit well with Al Malik. He was hurt and wanted to hurt me in turn. Little Head kept looking forlornly at me and shrugging his shoulders, making a face that conveyed his deep sympathy for his friend Al Malik and contempt for me, the interloper, traitor, and worse.

Al Malik then accused me of shaming him before his family because, he charged, I had tried to seduce one of his aunt's daughters. I was amazed, although another of the guides had warned me that Al Malik suspected me of this several days earlier. According to Al Malik, at the *usbu'a* for his brother's daughter, after all of the eating, trancing, and dancing, and before I was shown to my place to sleep among other members of the family, I had "spoken with" a woman (presumably the one I had noticed staring at me), and had made arrangements for a clandestine tryst with her. He even told me where I had planned to meet her, and at what time.

"Simply absurd," I remember thinking to myself as I sat there in the uncomfortable fluorescent glow of the café's back room. And yet, as he persisted I began to realize that I had been trapped, framed by Al Malik. With Little Head (who had not attended the *usbu'a*) present to witness Al Malik's indictment, and no one to support my denial, I would be judged guilty of sullying not only Al Malik's honor, but of showing disrespect to his entire family. There was nothing further to discuss. I had refused to pay him and now I refused to be intimidated by his fabricated accusation. Little Head shot me one more sidelong glance before he and Al Malik took their leave.

This was the last I ever saw of either of them.

Just as I had failed to gain access to the "purists" of a militant *umma* (because I could not fake a conversion to Islam), I lost access to the "opportunists" because I could not play the "game" of selling ersatz *objets d'art* at a usurious mark-up to my friends and family. The same rules of representation of self applied to each situation: essentially, outright lies are difficult to tell.

CHAPTER 21

Refractions of Reflections on Fieldwork in Morocco: Postmodernity, or the Sibylline

The inhabitants of the earth are of two sorts:
Those with brains, but no religion,
And those with religion, but no brains.

—ABU'L ALA' AL MA'ARRI, D. (1057)

"Where nothing is sacred, every belief becomes revisable."

—AHMED (1992:13)

Western culture has been diagnosed as being afflicted with a condition, which is fashionably called postmodernity. The word "modern" means *of or pertaining to the present time*; its Latin root *modo* which means *lately* or *just now* is joined with the adjective suffix *ernus*, which suggests *of time*. Thus, to be postmodern would imply being *after just now* or perhaps even *out of time*. Postmodernity has been called

> {C}onservative, consumer-oriented, cinematic and visual to the core...a masculinized culture of eros, love, desire, femininity, youth, and beauty. The postmodern person is a voyeur, someone who sits and gazes...{It} is a looking culture, organized in terms of a variety of gazes, or looks (e.g. tourist, investigatory—medical, social science, television, religious, political—artistic, photographic, etc.)

—DENZIN (1992:80)

Being "out of time" is rather hard to describe. The most common theme emerging from the literature is an emphasis upon the surfaces of social life, such as style and fashion (Featherstone, 1991; Harvey, 1989; Hebdige 1989). These ephemeral attributes are constitutive of reality, or are at least representative of what is thought to be commonly desired. The dominant metaphors are Disneyland and McDonald's (Ritzer 2000)

According to postmodern theorists, we are at the tipping point of either the creation of a new kind of society, or we are participant observers in what Harvey (1989:327–8) has called the cultural forms resulting from a "crisis of overaccumulation" in the capitalist economy beginning in the early 1970's. This condition is both wonderfully contemporary, and not at all "modern" — let alone postmodern. Resisting the urge to characterize an arbitrary increment of time as one thing or another, especially with an abstraction susceptible of reification like "postmodernism," I prefer the anthropologically grounded notion of an ambiguous mixture of "Magic, Science, and Religion" (Malinowski 1948), as simultaneously available to human beings as they negotiate their daily relationships with one another as well as with the physical world. Just as there is no "authenticity," there is no "postmodernity" — there are only relationships.

My time in Fez left me sympathetic to the antifoundationalist skepticism toward "theories of everything," and also of impartial objectivity. The claim that interpretations and expert authority are always partial at best, and contingent upon fluid social circumstances, strikes me as sound. My sympathy comes from my own experiences, and I am persuaded by the fundamental similarities that such suspicions — of Olympian impartiality, and of foundational truth-claims — share with social constructionism.

It is at this point, however, that I find postmodernist assertions less and less compelling. C.W. Mills (1959) argued that social science ought to aspire to provide "an adequate description of reality." Postmodernists' contention that the contingencies upon which scientific observations rest render those observations more apparent than real (Clifford and Marcus, 1986) is, at best, an abrogation of Mills' call for the practice of engaged social science. At worst, it seems to me that we are paralyzed or weakened considerably by a fascination with a philosophy of ambiguity which offers no protection from the casual "everyday brutality of cultural conformity" (Kipnis 1999) and the violence of daily life. By "protection" I mean that it is no longer enough to provide an adequate description of reality, and leave it at that—whatever "that" is.

Theories of modernity have emphasized close links between rising surplus, bureaucracy, science, and the market. What the full flower of modernity has revealed, however, is not the vanquishing of superstition, religion, or regional particularisms, et cetera, but rather a continuing persistence and occasional flare-ups of these "primitive" cultural attributes. This forces me to adopt a view that incorporates contingency as an alternative to the iron cage of functional integration.

"To move beyond the sterile antinomies of contemporary postmodernism requires that we summon the humility—and imagination—to entertain the possibility that earlier thinkers may have some insights worthy of our consideration" (Seaton 1999). If a term is necessary to characterize the times, I suggest "sibylline." According to the *Shorter Oxford English Dictionary* (2002) it means, "of or pertaining to the Sybil; oracular; exorbitant; excessive." It emphasizes the mystical qualities of prophesy, as well as the ambiguity of interpretation required to make sense of the oracle's utterances. By virtue of the association with ambiguity, the term leaves room for secular knowledge as well. This, then, is the sibylline era. It is a time of uncertainty and hubris.

The intellectual heritage of anthropology has by no means been rendered obsolete by postmodernist anti-foundational arguments about the fictive qualities of ethnography. The patient, systematic efforts to describe how people live will continue to be conducted, regardless of what some philosophically inclined anthropologists think and write. The people being written about know, or at least have some idea about, what they are doing and why they are doing it, and they are capable of talking about it. It is up to the anthropologist to be a student of behavior and meanings, and in this way to make the obscure lives and works of others part of a wider effort to describe and understand human society.

CHAPTER 22

So What?

Avalanche, veux-tu m'emporter dans ta chute?

—Charles Baudelaire

What is crucially at issue (and it is crucial at many levels, not the least of which is now being revealed in the events taking place in Iraq and Afghanistan) is the question of what, exactly, modernity entails. Is it inexorably "winner take all"—as many commentators have insisted, from Marx to the present—or are there viable alternatives? I have no definitive answer. The point is that it truly is an open question. If one were to look only at the "West," Japan, Korea, and China, it would appear that there is but one path: industrial capitalism. The remaining areas of ambiguity are to be found in the Middle East and Sub-Saharan Africa. Is there another way in these regions or is there only perpetual misery? Is there a way for a nation-state (or a culture) to claim with dignity to be neither fully committed to an industrialized future nor condemned to "underdevelopment"?

Short of extreme and dramatic efforts, Morocco will never be an industrial power on the order of South Korea or even Southern China. It will most likely remain oriented toward local production for local consumption, with some minor export-oriented industrial production (examples include Bata, Inc. athletic shoes, fashion leather garments, and the quasi-industrial production of blood oranges—though this is a seasonal product). What Euro-American industrially produced luxuries are imported into Moroccan society will be the fruit of fortunes reaped from tourism.

In short, Morocco is likely to remain largely an appendage to the consumer capitalism of the "developed" world. Is this a prescription for exploitation, self-abuse, disaster, or worse? It certainly is not a strategy for industrial economic development.

The Sharks fit into this discussion because they make their way by fulfilling the West's expectations of their being examples of orientalism, while at the same time being subversive of those expectations. They are a modernizing force in their society, if only because of their access to "easy" money and their proximity to affluent tourists. The Sharks operate in a context of expectations embedded in ambivalence.

One might reasonably ask, "Are the Sharks pimps or entrepreneurs?" At best, their "strategy" is one of self-exploitation. At worst their opportunism leaves the strong possibility of political tumult attractive, if only for the value of excitement that a riot can create. A volatile political arena affords opportunities for Islamicist radicals as well as thrill-seekers. Both groups of opportunists may conceivably "collaborate" to the detriment of all.

The *geeyad* I knew were in an ambiguous position, one about which they were profoundly ambivalent. They marketed the very aspects of their society they were endeavoring to escape. And yet, it is not at all clear that any of them wanted to "fully" escape. They all knew, if only vaguely, that were they to move to Asia, Europe, or the United States they would have to settle for menial jobs at best. In Fez, by contrast, they are far from being mere menial laborers.

My experience suggests that Morocco's ambitious bid to capture the lucrative international tourist market will fail, or short of that, "succeed" only by severe repression, if the young men (and, as seems increasingly likely, young women) who swell the ranks of eager guides to Morocco's "attractions" are not utilized in a productive manner consistent with their expectations of social mobility, fueled by Euro-American television, film, and advertising, as well as the relative extravagance of Western-style tourists. Indeed, how can their aspirations be accommodated when state-led economic growth no longer meets the expectations it was designed to address?

By manipulating orientalist expectations, the *geeyad* trade ersatz authenticity for cash. Their raucous resistance to the strictures of Islam, and the pleasure they take in breaking rules of behavior earn them a marginal place in society. At the same time the *geeyad* are making Morocco modern. If context defines deviance, then as Morocco embraces tourism, the Sharks and their contradictions might eventually cease to be seen as a threat to prosperity and the normative order. I see no reason why Islam cannot accommodate McWorld.

The *geeyad* were selling traditional culture to tourists and travelers who yearn for tradition, and mistakenly assume that with tradition comes authenticity. But, if one seeks authenticity, the developing world is probably the last place to look for it. Like the tourists and travelers I met, I was also in search of authenticity. But in Fez, I could not be inauthentic (disingenuous) when I was asked if I wanted to become a Muslim, yet while there I could become an authentic Shark. However, I could not be a Shark "back in the USA." Dishonesty is not particularly deviant in the United States; honesty is.

My experiences, inquiries, and ruminations in Morocco lead me to offer what amounts more to an observation than a conclusion. The New Crusades, as I have used the term, are not a Hobbesian "warre of each against all." Nor are they the "clash of civilizations," or of religions, as some have suggested. Rather, to judge from the men and women of Fez's medina whom I came to know, the New Crusades are less cause than effect; the result, rather than the catalyst, of unmet expectations.

These crusades are, therefore, not so much "against" as they are "for": for access to material comforts, leisure, pleasure, and the perceived freedom to consume. They are for, in a word, modernity. The New Crusades represent the success of advertising. Once they have been produced, products—tourist experiences included— must be sold. The desire to consume, to partake of the immense accumulation of products and services available to those who can afford them, has been created, enhanced, expanded, and exported. Morocco is simply one more market among many, even as it is packaged as a product. In short, the guides and many like them, coming from poor families, without education or opportunity for upward social mobility, are not content to remain passive in the midst of such potent perceptions of plenty. They too want their MTV. This is more profoundly disturbing to me than if poverty and desperation did indeed drive people to embrace a "retrograde" religious *weltanschauung*. But it does not. Instead people respond with alacrity, enthusiastically embracing the opportunity to buy the goods and services associated with Euro-American wealth, power, and leisure.

While leisure has long been a commodity, the industry associated with selling leisure services is fast-becoming one of the most powerful economic players in both local and international political struggles. The effects of the leisure industry are a "people spill" not unlike an oil spill. As a consumable "service good" leisure is contingent upon the violence that results from economic and political competition spreading from the site—or sites—of the tour itself, like concentric circles. The guides I knew are but one of these rings.

Poverty is not necessarily fanatic fundamentalism's incubator. If Fez becomes primarily a temple of consumption, the people who live there and earn their livelihoods by selling their culture may well not care very much, if at all, about the tourists' religion. Theirs is a domestic and secular crusade. Money too works in mysterious ways.

STUDY QUESTIONS

1. Why is Fez, Morocco an important location for anthropological research?

2. What is 'modernity'? What is 'tradition'? And what is the relationship between these two concepts?

3. What is the relationship between anthropological theory and Dizard's ethnography?

4. How does Dizard use anthropological theory to understand the people he studied?

5. What is the relationship between education, unemployment, and political/religious extremism in Morocco according to Dizard?

6. Who are the Sharks and what role do they play?

7. Why are the Sharks important people to understand?

8. What do the Sharks teach Dizard?

9. How did Dizard earn the confidence of those he studied?

10. Are there groups in American society comparable to the Sharks?

11. What made fieldwork so difficult for Dizard?

12. How does Dizard conceive of Authenticity?

13. What are the implications of Dizard's findings?

BIBLIOGRAPHY

ABC News
18 July 2002. "Poll: Most Americans say they're Christian." www.abcnews.com

Abu-Lughod, Janet L.
1980. *Rabat: Urban Apartheid in Morocco*. Princeton: Princeton University Press.
1989. *Before European Hegemony: The World System AD 1250–1350*. New York: Oxford University Press.

Abu-Rabi, Ibrahim
1995. *Intellectual Origins of Islamic Resurgence In the Modern Arab World*. New York: State University of New York Press.

Adil, B.
1993. *"Voyage dans l'univers d'un faux guide." L'Opinion*, p. 4. 1 December 1993.

Agnouch, Abdelatif
1987. *Histoire Politique du Maroc: Pouvoir, Légitimités, et Institutions*. Casablanca: Afrique Orient.

Ahmed, Akbar
1992. *Postmodernism and Islam: Predicament and Promise*. London: Routledge.

Ali, Ahmed, Tr.,
1984. *Al-Qur'an*. Princeton: Princeton University Press.

Alloula, Malek,
1988. *The Colonial Harem*. Wlad Godzich, Tr. Minneapolis: University of Minnesota Press.

Al Mahmoud, Abdul Latif
 2003. "Casablanca blasts a body blow to Morocco's struggling tourism." 19 May 2003. *The Peninsula: Qatar's Leading English Daily* www.thepeninsulaqatar.com.

Amrouche, Radhma and Dorothy Blair, Tr.,
 1988. *My Life Story: The Autobiography of a Berber Woman*. London: The Women's Press.

Anderson, Lisa
 1986. *The State and Social Transformation in Tunisia and Libya, 1830–1980*. Princeton: Princeton University Press.

Anonymous
 1994. From the journal of a traveler encountered in Morocco.

Ashford, Douglas
 1961. *Political Change in Morocco*. Princeton: Princeton University Press.
 1967. *National Development and Local Reform: Political Participation in Morocco, Tunisia and Pakistan*. Princeton: Princeton University Press.
 1973. "Second- and third-generation elites in the Maghrib." In I. William Zartman, ed., *Man, State, and Society in the Contemporary Maghrib*. Westport, CT: Praeger.

Atran, Scott
 2002. *In Gods We Trust: The Evolutionary Landscape of Religion*. New York: Oxford University Press.

Barakat, Halim
 1993. *The Arab World: Society, Culture, and State*. Berkeley: University of California Press.

Barber, Benjamin
 1996. *Jihad vs. McWorld: How Globalism and Tribalism Are Reshaping the World*. New York: Ballantine Books.

Barna Research Ltd
 2002. "The Bible: Beliefs." www.barna.org.

Basfao, Kacem and Jean-Robert Henry, eds.
1992. *Le Magreb, L'Europe et la France*. Paris: CNRS.

Baudelaire, Charles
1989 [1857]. *Les Fleurs du Mal*. Boston: David R. Godine.

Bentahar, Mekki
1988. *La Sociologie Marocaine Contemporaine: Bilan et Perspectives*. Rabat: Faculté des Lettres et des Sciences Humaines.

Berger, P. and Luckmann, T.
1967. *The Social Construction of Reality*. New York: Anchor Books.

Berman, Paul
2003. "The philosopher of Islamic terror." March 23rd, 2003. The New York Times Magazine. *The New York Times*.

Berreman, G.
1962. *Behind Many Masks: Ethnography and Impression Management in a Himalayan Village*. Ithaca, NYo: The Society for Applied Anthropology (Monograph no. 4).
1972. "Social categories and social interaction in urban India." *American Anthropologist*, 74 (3): 567–86.
1975. "Bazaar behavior: Social identity and social interaction in urban India," In: *Ethnic Identity: Cultural Continuities and Change*. George DeVos and Lola Romanucci-Ross, eds. Palo Alto, CA: Mayfield Publishing. Pp. 71–105.

Bey, Hakim
1999. *Overcoming Tourism*. Paris: Dissident Editions.

Blumer, Herbert
1969. *Symbolic Interactionism*. Englewood Cliffs: Prentice Hall.

Bourdieu, Pierre
1972. *Outline of a Theory of Practice*. New York: Cambridge University Press.

Bowen, Donna Lee and Evelyn Early
1993. *Everyday Life in the Muslim Middle East*. Bloomington: Indiana University Press.

Bowles, Paul
1955. *The Spider's House*. London: Peter Owen Ltd.
1989. *A Distant Episode: The Selected Stories*. Chicago: Ecco Press.
1991. Preface to William Betsch, *The Hakima: A Tragedy in Fez*. New York: Aperture Press.

Brand, Laurie
1998. *Women, the State, and Political Liberalization: Middle Eastern and North African Experiences*. New York: Columbia University Press.

Braverman, Harry
1975. *Labor and Monopoly Capital: the Degradation of Work in the Twentieth Century*. New York: Monthly Review Press.

Briggs, Jean
1970. *Never In Anger: Portrait of an Eskimo Family*. Cambridge: Harvard University Press.

British Broadcasting Corporation News
May 28, 2003. "Morocco suspect dies in custody."

Britton, Robert A.
1979. "The image of the third world in tourism marketing." *Annals of Tourism Research* 6 (1): 318–329.

Broad, W. J.
1986. *Star Warriors: A Penetrating Look Into the Lives of the Young Scientists Behind Our Space Age Weaponry*. New York: Simon and Schuster.

Browning, F.
1996. "Lost in Fez Morocco: The old city's medieval past comes alive in its narrow, labyrinthine streets." *The San Francisco Examiner*, Travel Section, pp. 1, 5, 6, 9. August 11, 1996.

Buck, Roy C.
1977. "The ubiquitous tourist brochure: Explorations in its intended and unintended use." *Annals of Tourism Research* 4 (4): 195–207.

Bumiller, Elizabeth and David Sanger
11 September 2002. "Threat of terrorism is shaping focus of Bush presidency." *The New York Times*.

Burke, Edmund III
1976. *Prelude to Protectorate in Morocco: Precolonial Protest and Resistance, 1860–1912*. Chicago: University of Chicago Press.

Burke, Edmund III and Ira Lapidus, eds.
1988. *Islam, Politics and Social Movements*. Berkeley: University of California Press.

Burkhardt, Titus
1999. *Fez, City of Islam*. London: I.B. Taurus & Co., Ltd.

Burns, Peter
1999. *An Introduction to Tourism and Anthropology*. New York: Routledge.

Bushnaq, Inea (ed. and trans.)
1986. *Arab Folktales*. New York: Pantheon.

Campanella, Tommaso
1623. Daniel Donno, Tr. (1981). *The City of the Sun: A Poetical Dialogue*. Berkeley: University of California Press.

Campbell, Patricia
1999. "Morocco in transition: Overcoming the democratic and human rights legacy of King Hassan II." *African Studies Quarterly* 7 (1):[online]
URL: http://web.africa.ufl.edu/asq/v7/v7i1a4.htm.

Céline, Louis-Ferdinand
1932 [1972]. *Voyage au Bout de la Nuit*. Paris: Gallimard.

Central Intelligence Agency (CIA)
2003. *The World Factbook: Morocco*. Washington, DC: United States Government Printing Office.

Chraïbi, Driss
1955. *Les Boucs*. Paris: Gallimard.

Clifford, J. and G. Marcus, eds.
1986. *Writing Culture: the Poetics and Politics of Ethnography*. Berkeley: University of California Press.

Cohen, Erik
1985. "The tourist guide: The origins, structure and dynamics of a role." In *Annals of Tourism Research*, 12: 5–29.

Colville, Major General Henry Edward
1884. *A Ride in Petticoats and Slippers: An Account of a Journey through Morocco*. London: Sampson Low, Marston, Searle & Rivington.

Combs-Schilling, M. E.
1989. *Sacred Performances: Islam, Sexuality, and Sacrifice*. New York: Columbia University Press.

Craib, I.
1984. *Modern Social Theory: From Parsons to Habermas*. Brighton: Wheatsheaf.

Crapanzano, Vincent
1973. *The Hamadsha: a Study in Moroccan Ethnopsychiatry*. Berkeley: University of California Press.

Denzin, Norman
1992. *Symbolic Interactionism and Cultural Studies: The Politics of Interpretation*. Oxford: Blackwell.

Doland, A.
2001. "Morocco's magic: Isolated mountains offer stunning peaks and an ancient culture." *The Eugene [Oregon] Register-Guard*. Travel Section, p. 3. October 7, 2001.

Duffy, Karen
  1983. "'Authenticity' and the contemporary Northwest coast Indian art market." *BC [British Columbia] Studies* 57: 99–111.

Duncan, J.S.
  1978. "The social construction of unreality: An interactionist approach to the tourist's cognition of environment." In D. Ley and M. Samuels, eds., *Humanistic Geography: Prospects and Problems*. London: Croom Helm.

Durrenberger, E. Paul and Suzan Erem
  1998. "When anthropology fails: Stories from the ethnographic front." *Anthropology and Humanism* 25 (1):50–63.

Duvignaud, Jean
  1970. *Change at Chebika: Report from a North African Village*. Austin: University of Texas Press.

Economist, The
  12/22/1990. "The fury in Fez." P. 42.
  3/23/1991. "Tourism in Morocco." P. 38.

Eickelman, Dale F.
  1975. *Moroccan Islam: Tradition and Society in a Pilgrimage Center*. Austin: University of Texas Press.
  1985. *Knowledge and Power in Morocco: The Education of a Twentieth-Century Notable*. Princeton: Princeton University Press.

Eisenstadt, S. N. and L. Roniger, eds.
  1984. *Patrons, Clients and Friends: Interpersonal Relations and the Structure of Trust in Society*. New York: Cambridge University Press.

Ellingson, Tore
  1997. "The evolution of bargaining behavior." *Quarterly Journal of Economics* Cambridge, MA: Harvard University Press. 112 (2): 581–602.

Entelis, John P.
   1989. *Culture and Counterculture in Moroccan Politics.* Boulder: Westview Press.

Errington, Frederick and Deborah Gewertz
   1989. "Tourism and anthropology in a post-modern world." *Oceania,* 60: 37–54.

Featherstone, M.
   1991. *Consumer Culture and Postmodernism.* Thousand Oaks: Sage.

Ferrell, J. and Mark Hamm, eds.
   1998. *Ethnography at the Edge: Crime, Deviance, and Field Research.* Chicago: Northeastern University Press.

Fine, Elizabeth and Jean Haskell Speer
   1981. "Tour guide performances as site sacralization." *Annals of Tourism Research* 12: 73–95.

Fischer, Michael and M. Abedi
   1990. *Debating Muslims.* Madison: University of Wisconsin.

Fleisher, Mark
   1995. *Beggars and Thieves: Lives of Urban Street Criminals.* Madison: University of Wisconsin.

Gardner, Sebastian
   1999. *Routledge Philosophy Guidebook to Kant and the Critique of Pure Reason.* New York: Routledge.

Garfinkel, Harold
   1967. *Studies In Ethnomethodology.* Englewood Cliffs, New Jersey: Prentice-Hall.

Garner, Bryan, ed.
   1999. *Black's Law Dictionary.* Eagan, MN: West Group.

Gerber, Jane
   1980. *Society in Fez: 1400–1700: Studies in Communal and Economic Life.* Leiden: Brill.

Geertz, Clifford.
　1971. *Islam Observed: Religious Development in Morocco and Indonesia*. Chicago: University of Chicago Press.
　1973. *The Interpretation of Cultures: Selected Essays*. New York: Basic Books.
　1979. *Meaning and Order in Moroccan Society*. New York: Cambridge University Press.
　1983. *Local Knowledge: Further Essays in Interpretive Anthropology*. New York: Basic Books.

Gellner, Ernest and Charles Micaud, eds.
　1972. *Arabs and Berbers: From the Tribe to Nation in North Africa*. Lanham, MD: Lexington Books.

Gellner, Ernest and John Waterbury, Eds.
　1977. *Patrons and Clients in Mediterranean Societies*. London: Duckworth Press.

Gellner, Ernest
　1981. *Muslim Society*. New York: Cambridge University Press.

Gewertz, Deborah and Frederick Errington
　1991. "We think, therefore they are? On occidentalizing the world." *Anthropological Quarterly* 64(2): 80–91.

Gilsenan, Michael
　1980. *Recognizing Islam*. New York: Pantheon.

Goffman, Erving
　1959. *The Presentation of Self in Everyday Life*. New York: Anchor Books.
　1963. *Behavior In Public Places*. Glencoe: The Free Press.
　1967. *Interaction Ritual: Essays On Face-To-Face Behavior*. Garden City, NY: Doubleday.

Goodstein, Laurie
　27 May 2003. "Seeing Islam as 'evil' gaith, Evangelicals seek converts." *The New York Times*.

Gorman, B.
　1979. "The Guided Tour: The Making of a Group." *Urban Life* 7(4): 469–92.

Graburn, Nelson H. H.
1995. "Tourism, modernity and nostalgia." In *The Future of Anthropology: Its Relevance to the Contemporary World*. Akbar S. Ahmed and Chris Shore, eds. London: The Athlone Press.

Gramsci, Antonio
1991. *Prison Notebooks, Volume 1*. New York: Columbia University Press.

Hammoudi, Abdallah.
1993. *The Victim and its Masks*. Chicago: University of Chicago Press.
1997. *Master and Disciple: The Cultural Foundations of Moroccan Authoritarianism*. Chicago: University of Chicago Press.

Handler, Richard and Jocelyn Linnekin
1989. "Tradition, genuine or spurious." In Elliot Oring, ed., *Folk Groups and Folklore Genres: A Reader*. Logan: Utah State University Press.

Harvey, David
1989. *The Condition of Postmodernity*. Oxford: Blackwell.

Hayes, D.
October 1994. "To be in Morocco is to enter the realm of the senses." *Jax Fax Travel Marketing Magazine*.

Hebdige, Dick
1989. *Hiding in the Light: On Images and Things*. London: Methuen.

Helprin, Mark
1992. *A Soldier of the Great War*. New York: Avon Books.

Hobsbawm, Eric
1994. *The Age of Extremes*. New York: Vintage.

Hodges, Tony
1983. *Western Sahara: The Roots of a Desert War*. Chicago: Lawrence Hill.

Holloway, J. Christopher
1981. "The guided tour: A sociological approach." *Annals of Tourism Research*, VIII (3): 377–402.

Horne, Alistair
1977. *A Savage War of Peace: Algeria 1954–1962*. New York: Penguin.

Hourani, Albert
1997. *History of the Arab Peoples*. Cambridge: Harvard University Press.

Hugh of Saint Victor, Jerome Taylor, Trans.
1991[1130]. *The Didascalicon of Hugh of Saint Victor: A Medieval Guide to the Arts*. New York: Columbia University Press.

Hulme, Katherine
1930. *Arab Interlude*. Philadelphia: Macrea, Smith Co.

Hull, Alistair, Jose Wyhowska and Nicolas Barnard
2000. *Kilim, The Complete Guide: History, Pattern, Technique, Identification*. San Francisco: Chronicle Books.

Humphreys, Andrew
2003. "Stars flock to the land of forbidden pleasure." *The Observer*. London: The Guardian, Ltd.

Huntington, Samuel P.
1998. *The Clash of Civilizations and the Remaking of World Order*. Carmichael, CA: Touchstone Books.

Ibaaquil, Larbi
1996. *L'école Marocaine et la Compétition Sociale: Stratégies, Aspirations*. Rabat: Babil.

Jackson, J.B.
1980. *The Necessity for Ruins and Other Topics*. Amherst: University of Massachusetts Press.

Jackson, P.
1985. "Urban ethnography" *Progress in Human Geography* 9: 157–76.

Joffé, George
 1992. "The changing geography of North Africa: Development, migration and the demographic time bomb." In Graham Chapman and Kathleen Baker, eds., *The Changing Geography of Africa and the Middle East*. New York: Routledge.
 1993. Ed. *North Africa: Nation, State, and Region*. New York: Routledge.

Jameson, Fredric
 1983. "Postmodernism and consumer society." In Foster, ed. 1983. *The Anti-Aesthetic: Essays on Postmodern Culture*. Port Townsend, WA: Bay Press. Pp. 111–125.
 1984. "Postmodernism, or the cultural logic of late capitalism." *New Left Review* 146: 53–92.

Johnson-Davies, Denys, Trans.
 1983. *Arabic Short Stories*. Berkeley: University of California Press.

Kaplan, Robert
 1996. *The Ends of the Earth: A Journey to the Frontiers of Anarchy*. New York: Random House.

Kent, Linda
 1992. "Fieldwork that failed." In Philip DeVita, ed. (1992). *The Naked Anthropologist*. Pp. 17–26.

Kepel, Gilles
 1994. *The Revenge of God: The Resurgence of Islam, Christianity, and Judaism in the Modern World*. University Park, PA: Penn State University Press.
 2002. *Jihad: The Trail of Political Islam*. Cambridge, MA: Harvard University Press.

Kepel, Gilles and Yann Richard, Eds.
 1990. *Intellectuels et Militants de l'Islam Contemporain*. Paris: Seuil.

Khair-Eddine, Mohammed
 1984. *Legende et Vie d'Agoun'chich*. Paris: Seuil.

Khatibi, Abdelkebir
   1983. *Amour Bilangue*. Paris: Fata Morgana.

Kipnis, Laura
   1999. *Bound and Gagged: Pornography and the Politics of Fantasy in America*. Durham, NC: Duke University Press.

Kirshenblatt-Gimblett, Barbara
   1987. "Authenticity and authority in the representation of culture: The poetics and politics of tourist production." In *Kulturkontakt Kulturkonflikt*. IKEE: Universität Frankfurt am Main. Pp. 59–69.

Kirshenblatt-Gimblett, Barbara and Edward M. Bruner
   1989. "Tourism." In the *International Encyclopedia of Communications*, vol. 4. Oxford: Oxford University Press. Pp. 249–253.

Kraus, J. Robin
   2001. "Charmed by Morocco in a Wink: Just when you think your pocket is being picked, it's your heart that is stolen." *The New York Times*, Travel Section, p. 23. August 19, 2001.

Krueger, Alan and Jitka Maleckova
   2002. "The economics and the education of suicide bombers: Does poverty cause terrorism?" *The New Republic*.

Ksikes, Driss
   1994. *"35% des logements en ville, précaires et illégaux."* La Libération, no. 997, p. 1. Casablanca.

Kuletz, V.
   1998. *The Tainted Desert: Environmental and Social Ruin in the American West*. New York: Routledge.

Lamchichi, Abderrahim
   1997. *Le Maghreb Face à l'Islamisme: Le Maghreb entre Tentations Autoritaires, essor de l'Islamisme et Demandes Démocratiques*. Paris: Harmattan.

Lapidus, Ira
1988. *History of Islamic Societies*. New York: Cambridge University Press.
1983. *Contemporary Islamic Movements in Historical Perspective*. Berkeley: University of California Press.

Laroui, Abdallah
1977. *The History of the Maghrib: An Interpretive Essay*. Princeton: Princeton University Press.

Le Matin du Sahara
1984. "*Niveaux de croyance parmi les citoyens du royaume.*" Casablanca.

Le Tourneau, R.
1961. *Fez In the Age of the Marinides*. Norman: University of Oklahoma.

Let;s Go: Spain, Portugal and Morocco
1991. Cambridge: Harvard Student Agencies.

Leveau, Rémy
1976. *Le Fellah Marocain, Défenseur du Trône*. Paris: Presses de la Fondation Nationale des Sciences Politiques.

Levi-Strauss, Claude
1974. *Tristes Tropiques*. New York: Athenaeum.

Ley, D.
1981. "Behavioural geography and the philosophies of meaning." In K.R. Cox and R.G. Golledge, eds., *Behavioural Problems in Geography Revisited*. London: Methuen.

Leymarie, Serge and Jean Tripier
1992. *Maroc: Le Prochain Dragon?* Casablanca: EDDIF.

Löfgren, Orvar
1999. *On Holiday: A History of Vacationing*. Berkeley: University of California Press.

Ma'aari, Abu'l Ala al
1984. In Amin Maalouf, *The Crusades Through Arab Eyes*. London: Al Saqi Books. P. 37.

Maa El Ainain, Charii
   1990. *Demographie Marocaine: Sources des Données et Caracteristiques d'Evolution.* Rabat: Centre d'Etudes et de Recherches Demographiques.

Maalouf, Amin
   1984. *The Crusades Through Arab Eyes*. London: Al Saqi Books.

MacCannell, Dean
   1989. *The Tourist: A New Theory of the Leisure Class*. New York: Schoken Press.
   1992. *Empty Meeting Grounds: The Tourist Papers*. New York: Routledge.

Maghreb arabe Presse
   2003. "No Islamic extremism threat looms." Paris: MAP.

Malinowski, Bronislaw
   1948. *Magic, Science and Religion, and Other Essays*. Boston: Beacon Press.

Mansouri, Mohammed
   1988. "Moroccan tourism image in France." *Annals of Tourism Research* 15 (4).

Maran, Rita
   1989. *Torture: The Role of Ideology in the French-Alerian War*. Westport, CT: Praeger.

Marx, Karl
   1977. *A Contribution to the Critique of Political Economy*. (1859). Moscow: Progress Publishers.

Mattson, James
   1971. "Development in the Arab World." In Mark Tessler, ed. (1982). *A New Look at the Middle East: Proceedings of a Conference at the University of Wisconsin-Milwaukee*. Milwaukee: Institute of World Affairs.

Maxwell, Gavin
   1966. *Lords of the Atlas: The Rise and Fall of the House of Glaoua, 1893–1956*. New York: Longman Press.

McKean, Philip F.
1973. *Cultural Involution: Tourists, Balinese and the Process of Modernization in an Anthropological Perspective*. Ph.D. dissertation. Brown University.

McMurray, David
2001. *In and Out of Morocco*. Minneapolis: University of Minnesota Press.

McNeil, John Robert
1992. "Kif in the Rif: An Historical and Ecological Perspective on Marijuana, Markets, and Manure in Northern Morocco." *Mountain Research and Development* 12(4): 389–92.

McRoberts, Duncan McCallum
2002. "Tradition and modernity." *Katarxis* 2:1. www.katarxis.com.

Mead, George Herbert
1934. *Mind, Self and Society*. Chicago: Chicago University Press.

Mernissi, Fatima
1987. *Beyond the Veil: Male-Female Dynamics in Modern Muslim Society*. Bloomington: Indiana University Press.
1992. *Islam and Democracy: Fear of the Modern World*. Boston: Addison Wesley.

Mezzine, Mohamed
1992. *Fès medievale: entre légènde et histoire, un Carrefour de l'Orient a l'apogée d'un rêve*. Paris: Editions Autrement, Série Mémoires 13.

Middle East North Africa Financial Network
2003. "Moody's changes Morocco's outlook to stable from negative." June 19th, 2003. www.menafn.com.

Mills, C. Wright
1959. *The Sociological Imagination*. New York: Oxford University Press.

Mimouni, Rachid
1993. *La Malédiction*. Casablanca: EDDIF.

Misheva, Vessela
2000. *Shame and Guilt: Sociology as a Poietic System.* Uppsala: Uppsala University Sweden.

Morocco
1998. Victoria, Australia: Lonely Planet Publications.

Moussalli, Ahmad
1993. *Radical Islamic Fundamentalism: The Ideological and Political Discourse of Sayyid Qutb.* Syracuse: Syracuse University Press.

Munson, Henry Jr.
1993. *Religion and Power in Morocco.* New Haven: Yale University Press.

Nedelcovych, M. and Monte Palmer
1982. "The university and the radicalization of disenfranchised youth: A case study of Moroccan university students." *Journal of South Asian and Middle Eastern Studies* 6: 267–284.

New York Times
27 May 2003. "Seeing Islam as 'evil' faith, evangelicals seek converts." Page 1.

Nomani, Farhad and Ali Rahnema
1994. *Islamic Economic Systems.* London: Zed Books.

Office Nationale Marocaine du Tourisme
2000. http://www.tourisme-marocain.com.

Ossman, Susan
1994. *Picturing Casablanca: Portraits of Power in a Moroccan City.* Berkeley: University of California Press.

Oussaid, Brik
1983. *Mountains Forgotten By God.* Washington, DC: Three Continents Press.

Parker, Richard
1984. *North Africa: Regional Tensions and Strategic Concerns.* Westport, CT: Praeger.

Pascon, Paul and Mekki Bentahar
1972. *"Ce que dissent 296 jeunes ruraux."* In *Etudes Sociologiques sur le Maroc*. Abdelkebir Khatibi, ed. Rabat: Bulletin Economique et Social du Maroc.

Pearce, Philip L.
1977. "Mental souvenirs: A study of tourists and their city maps." *Australian Journal of Psychology* 29: 203–210.
1982. *The Social Psychology of Tourist Behavior*. Oxford: Pergamon Press.

Petersen, Andrew
1996. *The Dictionary of Islamic Architecture*. New York: Routledge.

Pi-Sunyer, Oriol
1981. "Tourism and anthropology." *Annals of Tourism Research* VIII (2): 271–284.

Porch, Douglas
1982. *The Conquest of Morocco*. New York: Alfred Knopf.

Porphyrios, Demitri
2002. "Tradition and modernity." *Katarxis* 2:1. www.katarxis.com.

Pred, Allan and Michael Watts
1992. *Reworking Modernity*. Piscataway, NJ: Rutgers University Press.

Prochaska, David
1990. *Making Algeria French: Colonialism in Bône, 1870–1920*. New York: Cambridge University Press.

Pruitt, Deborah
1993. *Foreign Mind: Tourism, Identity and Development in Jamaica*. Doctoral dissertation, University of California, Berkeley.

Qutb, Seyd
1981. *Milestones [Maalim fi al-Tariq]*. (S. Badrul Hassan, trans.) Karachi: International Islamic Publishers.

Rabinow, Paul.
1975. *Symbolic Domination: Cultural Form and Historical Change in Morocco*. Chicago: University of Chicago Press.
1977. *Reflections on Fieldwork in Morocco*. Chicago: University of Chicago Press.
1986. "Representations are social facts." In *Writing Culture: The Poetics and Politics of Ethnography*. (James Clifford and George E. Marcus, eds.) Berkeley: University of California Press. Pp. 234–261.

Ranger, T.O., ed.
1992. *The Invention of Tradition*. New York: Cambridge University Press.

Redfoot, Donald R.
1984. "Touristic authenticity, touristic angst, and modern reality." *Qualitative Sociology* 7: 4.

Redman, Charles
1986. *Qsar-es-seghir*. Orlando, FL: Academic Press.

Rejali, Darius
1994. *Torture and Modernity: Self, Society, and State in Modern Iran*. Boulder: Westview Press.

Richards, Alan and John Waterbury
1990. *A Political Economy of the Middle East: State, Class, and Economic Development*. Boulder: Westview Press.

Ritter, W.
1975. "Recreation and tourism in Islamic countries." *Existics* 236: 56–9.

Ritzer, G.
2000. *The McDonaldization of Society*. Thousand Oaks: Pine Forge Press.

Rock, P. and David Downes
1985. *Understanding Deviance: A Guide to the Sociology of Crime and Rule Breaking*. London: Oxford University Press.

Rosenthal, Franz
1971. *The Herb: Hashish versus Medieval Society*. Leiden: Brill.

Rotenberg, Robert and Gary McDonogh, eds.
1993. *The Cultural Meaning of Urban Space*. Westport: Bergin and Garvey.

Roy, Olivier
1994. *The Failure of Political Islam*. (Carol Volk, Trans.) Cambridge: Harvard University Press.

Ryan, C.
1991. *Recreational Tourism: A Social Science Perspective*. London: Routledge.

Said, Edward
1978. *Orientalism*. Westport, CT: Praeger.
1997. *Covering Islam*. New York: Vintage Books

Sanoussi, Ahmed
1995. "The ink of my heart." In C. Hedges, "Jokes from underground keep Morocco laughing." *The New York Times*, 21 February 1995. p. 4.

Seaton, James
1999. "The metaphysics of postmodernism." *Humanitas* XII(1):.

Segal, Eliezer
1981. "The oral law ... the Mishnah," in: I. Gottlieb [et al], *Jerusalem to Jabneh*. Tel Aviv: Everyman's University.

Shahin, Emad Eldin
1998. *Political Ascent: Contemporary Islamic Movements in North Africa*. Boulder: Westview Press.

Silverman, Debora.
1986. *Selling Culture: Bloomingdale's, Diana Vreeland, and the New Aristocracy of Taste in Reagan's America*. New York: Pantheon.

Sitwell, Sacheverell
1940. *Mauretania: Warrior, Man, and Woman*. London: Duckworth.

Shils, Edward
 1981. *Tradition*. Chicago: University of Chicago Press.

Smith, Valene
 1977. *Hosts and Guests: The Anthropology of Tourism*. Philadelphia: University of Pennsylvania Press.

Sprinzak, Ehud
 2000. "Rational fanatics." *Foreign Policy*. Washington, DC: Carnegie Endowment for International Peace.

Suleiman, Michael W.
 1985. "Socialization to politics in Morocco: Sex and regional factors." *International Journal of Middle East Studies*, 17: 313–327.
 1987. "Attitudes, values and the political process in Morocco." In *The Political Economy of Morocco*, I. William Zartman, ed. Westport, CT: Praeger.

Swearingen, Will D.
 1987. *Moroccan Mirages: Agrarian Dreams and Deceptions, 1912–1986*. Princeton: Princeton University Press.

Taylor, Lucien and Ilisa Barbash
 1992. *In and Out of Africa.* Video. Berkeley: University of California Extension Center For Media and Independent Learning.

Tessler, Mark
 1982. "Morocco: Institutional Pluralism and Monarchical Dominance." In I. William Zartman, et al. *Political Elites in Arab North Africa*. New York: Longman.
 1985. "The uses and limits of populism: The political strategy of King Hassan II of Morocco," *Middle East Review* (Spring 1985): 47–66.
 1993. "Alienation of Urban Youth." In *Polity and Society in Contemporary North Africa*, Zartman and Habeeb, eds. Boulder: Westview Press. Pp. 71–101.

Thomas, David Hurst
 2001. *Skull Wars: Kennewick Man, Archaeology, and the Battle for Native American Identity*. New York: Basic Books.

Tierney, Patrick
2000. *Darkness In El Dorado: How Scientists and Journalists Devastated the Amazon*. New York: W.W. Norton.

Tomlinson, John
1991. *Cultural Imperialism: A Critical Introduction*. Baltimore: Johns Hopkins University Press.

Tozy, Mohammed
1984. *Champ et Contre-Champ Politico-Religieux au Maroc*. Cited in Entelis, *Culture and Counterculture in Moroccan Politics* (1989:79–87 *passim*).
1993. "Islam and the State." In *Polity and Society in Contemporary North Africa*, Zartman and Habeeb, eds. Boulder: Westview. Pp. 102–122.
1999. *Monarchie et Islam Politique au Maroc.* Paris: Presses de Sciences Politique.

Trumble et al.
2002. *The Shorter Oxford English Dictionary*. New York: Oxford University Press.

Turner, Bryon S.
1994. *Orientalism, Post-Modernism and Globalism*. London: Routledge.

United Nations Demographic Yearbook
1990. New York: United Nations.

UNESCO Statistical Yearbook
1976, 1983, 1986, 1988. New York: United Nations.

Urry, John
1990. *The Tourist Gaze*. London: Sage Publications.

Veblen, Thorstein
1994. *The Theory of the Leisure Class*. (1899) New York: Penguin Books.

Waterbury, John.
1970. *The Commander of the Faithful: the Moroccan Political Elite - A Study in Segmented Politics*. New York: Columbia University Press.

Wehr, Hans [J.M. Cowan, ed.]
1980. *A Dictionary of Modern Written Arabic*. Beirut: Librarie du Liban.

Widmer-Münch, Roland
1990. *Der Tourismus in Fès und Marrakech: Strukturen und Prozesse in bipolaren Urbanräumen des islamischen Orients*. Basel: Geographische Institut der Universität Basel.

Wilmsen, Edwin
1989. *Land Filled With Flies: A Political Economy of the Kalahari*. Chicago: University of Chicago Press.

Wolf, Margery
1992. *A Thrice-Told Tale: Feminism, Postmodernism, and Ethnographic Responsibility*. Palo Alto: Stanford University Press.

Woolman, David
1968. *Rebels in the Rif: Abd el Krim and the Rif Rebellion*. Palo Alto: Stanford University Press.

World Development Report
1992. Washington, DC: World Bank.

World Travel and Tourism Council
www.wttc.travel

www.ArabicNews.com
2000. "Colloquium on Morocco between tradition and modernity held in Marrakech." 19 June 2000.

www.lectlaw.com
2002. "Tradition." *Bouvier's Legal Dictionary*.

Youell, Raymond
    1998. *Tourism: An Introduction*. Boston: Pearson Higher Education.

Zartman, I. William, ed.
    1982. *Political Elites in Arab North Africa*. New York: Longman.
    1987. *The Political Economy of Morocco*. Westport, CT: Praeger.
    1993. Zartman and Habeeb eds. *Polity and Society in Contemporary North Africa*. Boulder: Westview

Zerrouky, Hassane
    2003. "*Au Maroc, l'Islamisme Prospère.*" *Courrier International* 22/05/2003, *Numéro* 655 Algiers: *Le Matin*.

www.ingramcontent.com/pod-product-compliance
Lightning Source LLC
Chambersburg PA
CBHW070332230426

43663CB00011B/2288